Praise for *Ca*

I've been trying to find the right words to express how much *Call Me Vivian* changed the course of my life. I'm convinced that God spoke to me through Katie's book. It brought me closer to God, gave me hope, restored my faith, and gave me the strength to press on during a very dark season. Since reading her book, I have been on a wonderful journey of recovery. I can't thank Katie enough for her inspiration.

> Alisa Johns Snow, former inmate, Oklahoma

Call Me Vivian renewed my hope! God showed me through her story that he is with me and will never leave or forsake me. Katie's book confirmed everything that I believe and everything that God needed me to know about his love for us.

> Alan Marie Lopez, inmate, Texas

I was blessed with the opportunity to read *Call Me Vivian*. Katie gave me something to strive for and helped me learn to forgive myself. I would like to thank Katie for her courage, faith, and continued work, not only in spreading God's Word, but also her dedication to helping inmates and children of incarcerated parents.

> Jessica Marie Flanders, inmate, Florida

Call Me Vivian encouraged me and renewed my hope during my incarceration. I pray that God will bless The Vivian Foundation and Katie's ministry work as she continues to bless those in need. Thank you—from the depths of my soul—for all you do to help others.

> Selena Ball, former inmate, Texas

Something about Katie Scheller's story has touched my soul. I was blessed to have found her book at a time when I needed it most.

> Racheal Parizek, inmate, North Dakota

Call Me Vivian is a powerful, powerful book. Katie beat the odds. Very few people bounce back from what she had been through and where she has been. I would like to thank Katie for her endless devotion to God and for making the world a better place.

Therrold James, inmate, Louisiana

God placed *Call Me Vivian* in my hands. It's a beautiful testimony and an amazing story about being blessed with the Holy Spirit. God is the only way anyone is ever going to succeed in life, as evidenced by Katie's experience.

Sonya Kennedy, inmate, Washington

Call Me Vivian is inspired by the Holy Spirit of God. Thank you for this wonderful book, which has been a blessing to my life.

Vivian Corujo Rojas, inmate, Texas

I loved Katie's book and story. It was very touching. Her story made me laugh and cry. It also inspired and strengthened me during a time when I really needed it.

Jacqueline Graham, inmate, Texas

Call Me Vivian has greatly affected me, and I am so appreciative of Katie's story. God, indeed, knows what he is doing and how to use his disciples. Thank you to all who made this book possible. God is using it to speak to people and encourage them.

Jennifer Michalka, inmate, Colorado

I would like to thank Katie for sharing her life story in *Call Me Vivian*. She is called and blessed by God to seek and do his will. I can't imagine having been through all that she has, yet she took destruction and made it beautiful by humbly walking God's path. It is my treasure and blessing to know of the work that she is doing through The Vivian Foundation.

Marilyn Brasher, ministry volunteer, Florida

Vivian's Call

A Labor of Love

KATIE SCHELLER

BroadStreet
PUBLISHING

BroadStreet Publishing® Group, LLC
Savage, Minnesota, USA
BroadStreetPublishing.com

Vivian's Call: A Labor of Love

Copyright © 2022 Katie Scheller
978-1-4245-6260-2 (paperback)
978-1-4245-6261-9 (e-book)

This book is a memoir. It reflects the author's present recollections of experiences over time. Some names and characteristics have been changed, some events have been compressed, and some dialogue has been recreated.

Unless noted otherwise, all Scripture quotations are taken from the Holy Bible, New Living Translation. Copyright © 1996, 2004, 2015 by Tyndale House Foundation. Used by permission of Tyndale House Publishers, a Division of Tyndale House Ministries, Carol Stream, Illinois 60188. All rights reserved. Scripture quotations marked TPT are from The Passion Translation®. Copyright © 2017, 2018 by Passion & Fire Ministries, Inc. Used by permission. All rights reserved. ThePassionTranslation.com. Scripture quotations marked NIV are taken from The Holy Bible, New International Version® NIV®. Copyright © 1973, 1978, 1984, 2011 by Biblica, Inc.™ Used by permission. All rights reserved worldwide. Scripture quotations marked ESV are taken from the ESV® Bible (The Holy Bible, English Standard Version®). Copyright © 2001 by Crossway, a publishing ministry of Good News Publishers. Used by permission. All rights reserved. Scripture quotations marked (GNT) are taken from the Good News Translation in Today's English Version— Second Edition. Copyright © 1992 by American Bible Society. Used by Permission.

Stock or custom editions of BroadStreet Publishing titles may be purchased in bulk for educational, business, ministry, fundraising, or sales promotional use. For information, please email orders@broadstreetpublishing.com.

Author photo by Jeff Rogers at Jeff Rogers Photography, Inc.

Design and typesetting by Garborg Design Works | garborgdesign.com

Printed in China

22 23 24 25 26 5 4 3 2 1

This book is dedicated to everyone who has answered God's call.

For my children and grandchildren:

Mike, Jenny, Brian,

Nicholas, Benjamin, Colin,

Landon, Tyler, and McKenzie

Let us run with endurance
the race God has set before us.

Hebrews 12:1

Praise the Lord, you angels, you mighty ones who carry out his plans, listening for each of his commands. Yes, praise the Lord, you armies of angels who serve him and do his will!

Psalm 103:20–21

Contents

Prologue

s I boarded a plane to Raleigh, North Carolina, I clearly heard
God say, *It's time to be bold.* Then he spoke Joshua 1:9, "This
is my command—be strong and courageous! Do not be afraid or
discouraged. For the LORD your God is with you wherever you go."
I didn't know what to think. The last time God had shared that
verse with me was during the most difficult time of my former
incarceration.

On behalf of Forgiven Ministry, a partner of The Vivian
Foundation, of which I am the president and CEO, I was flying to
the North Carolina Correctional Institution for Women to serve as
a guest speaker. Forgiven Ministry hosts a camp called "One Day
with God," in which imprisoned parents reunite with their children. It is a divinely appointed time for both the children and the
inmates to experience the love of God, find forgiveness, and recon-
cile as a family.

I was thrilled by the invitation, and it was apparent that everything the Lord had told me to do regarding my ministry work was
coming together at the perfect time. Something unexpected was
sure to happen since God had spoken Joshua 1:9 to me a second
time. As a former inmate who served time at the largest federal
prison in United States, I wondered what North Carolina's largest
facility would be like since it housed female offenders of all levels.

Days later, I spoke to forty inmates who would reunite with
their children the following morning. I also visited the compound's
infirmaries and spent time with hospitalized individuals, and by
that evening, I would return to the podium to speak to the general
population. But as I was leaving the second infirmary with Scottie

Barnes, the woman in charge of Forgiven Ministry and "One Day with God," she casually mentioned that we had one more place to stop before I returned to the event and spoke to the general population. "Katie," she said, "it's time to visit death row."

I questioned whether my heart was ready to handle such an assignment. Sure, I had witnessed quite a lot throughout my life's journey. Countless tears, much-needed laughter, and continually answered prayers filled my life. While God had also shown me a lot, the magnitude of watching the door to death row open told me that I still had much to learn.

We entered the building that held the death row inmates and stepped inside an elevator. I had no idea what to expect, but I took a deep breath. After exiting the elevator, we walked down the white, cement brick hallway with its freshly polished floor toward two guards seated at their command post. After we went through the prison's security protocol, one steel door opened and closed, and then another. I silently prepared myself to meet three women sentenced to death for their crimes.

We introduced ourselves, and each woman, clad in a maroon prison jumpsuit, greeted me. My eyes cautiously looked beyond the spot where we stood in order to survey the women's living quarters: seven cells, a common area used for eating and visiting, and a small, secure concrete patio that the inmates were permitted to use for one hour each day. Their living space overlooked the chapel.

All three women were murderers, but that did not matter in the moment. God wanted me to see them through the eyes of Jesus. No judgment, no condemnation, only unconditional love, for "perfect love casts out fear" (1 John 4:18). Each ministry moment that day required a significant amount of energy, and when the time came for my evening speech, I was running on empty. I had no choice but to turn things over to the Holy Spirit.

Little did I know that the next day would be equally demanding. I met with a former death row inmate whose sentence was commuted to life in prison, and she had quite a story to share with me. Would it surprise you to learn that a coloring book donated by The Vivian Foundation saved this prisoner's life?

God had begun to show me the fruit of my labor. He was doing amazing things in me, for me, and through me. In his infinite wisdom, he guided me. In his infinite power, he protected me. In his infinite grace, he carried me. More importantly, in his infinite love, he showed me the miraculous work he can accomplish with a willing heart.

As Jeremiah 29:11 reads, " 'For I know the plans I have for you,' says the LORD. 'They are plans for good and not disaster, to give you a future and a hope.' " *Vivian's Call,* the sequel to *Call Me Vivian*, is a demonstration of God's power that proves we can make our own plans, but God's purpose will prevail as he lovingly guides our steps.

1

The sins of my past vanished along with the heartache and pain that came with them. My sanctification required 740 days served in prison, $400,000 paid in restitution, one year of probation, and countless hours spent at the computer. God's plan was coming together at the perfect time.

As my first book, *Call Me Vivian,* went to print and distribution, I wondered how I would react to seeing it and holding it. When the book finally arrived on my doorstep six weeks prior to its launch date, I felt like a little kid at Christmas. A wide smile appeared on my face, and I flipped the book over to admire the back cover, which read,

> *Call Me Vivian* is a true story about a woman caught up in adultery. On the fast track in Corporate America, Katie became involved in an illicit love affair with her boss that newspapers reported as "sordid." Not everyone's extramarital affair makes front page news or results in a civil lawsuit or criminal charges that land a person in federal prison. But hers did.
>
> From a financially secure future to losing everything except her positive attitude, sense of humor, and faith, Katie found herself sleeping on the concrete floor in a prison cell she describes as "one step above hell." It was in this place that God did His best work!

This book exposes the truth about Katie's struggle with sexual sin, the battle for her heart, and the transforming power of God's love. Through Katie's heartache, pain, and countless years of searching, you will gain a better understanding of God's wonderful gifts of grace and forgiveness.

Call Me Vivian will prove all things are possible with God if you simply have the faith to believe.

As I prepared the manuscript for *Call Me Vivian*, a woman, who had no idea that I was called to be an author, spoke prophetic words to me. We were praying together one afternoon when she placed her hands on my forehead. I tangibly felt God's power radiate throughout my entire body as she spoke.

"Books, books, books," she said. "I see many books. Some of them are already in the library of heaven. The Holy Spirit will write these, and you are the vessel. You are to write from your heart, not your head. God will give you dreams and visions. Be ready to write."

Sure enough, I heard whispers from heaven virtually every day while I penned *Call Me Vivian*. God miraculously guided each keystroke, creating an effortless writing process. I wish I could say the same thing about my personal journey. Unfortunately, I endured a tumultuous period as a defendant in a civil lawsuit and criminal proceedings, all of which played out well over a decade. But every bit of my heartache and pain was necessary for God to prepare my heart for his ultimate calling on my life.

While finishing *Call Me Vivian* in 2015, I had numerous opportunities to share my testimony. I also researched firms and agencies that promoted authors. The amount of money bestselling authors could earn through speaking engagements shocked me. But the famous last words of the apostle Paul rang in my ears: "It is the opportunity to preach the Good News without charging anyone. That's why I never demand my rights when I preach the Good News" (1 Corinthians 9:18). By day, Paul worked as a tentmaker. By night, he spread the good news about Jesus, never demanding pay for his evening assignment. God gave me similar marching orders; part of my ministry calling was to give my book away.

I prepared for the book's launch by scheduling newspaper, radio, and television interviews. I also continued to put the finishing touches on The Vivian Foundation, the 501(c)(3) certified nonprofit organization I had started to share God's love with inmates and children of incarcerated parents. The Vivian Foundation also provides Christian resources to other organizations dedicated to helping these families. The Vivian Foundation's logo design, website, and marketing tools were finalized, and our first event, a conference hosted by the Correctional Ministries and Chaplain's Association, was scheduled for May of 2016 in Atlanta.

While Skyping with my Bible study group one evening, we talked about the upcoming conference. For many years, a member of our small group had been saying that she had experienced recurring visions of operating merchandise tables at these types of events. At virtually the same time, all three friends in my Bible study said, "Katie, you need to secure a credit card reader for upcoming merchandise and book sales." I couldn't help but laugh to myself since only days earlier God had instructed me not to charge anyone.

The next day I headed out to do a little Christmas shopping but first visited my bank to withdraw cash. I figured I might as well inquire about credit card device readers since I was already there, but the banker I usually worked with was busy. As another employee walked by, I stopped him to ask a quick question, but he, too, was busy with another customer. I took a seat in the lobby, and within a few minutes, a third banker, Joe, asked if he could help me. I stepped into his office not realizing that God had me right where he wanted me.

Joe and I started talking, and while I shared tidbits about *Call Me Vivian* and The Vivian Foundation, it became apparent that Joe was also a Christian. I openly shared my testimony and told him about my upcoming speaking engagements. He told me about local prison ministries in western Racine County in Wisconsin. I can't remember how it came up, but I told him that I had asked a local car dealership if their corporate headquarters could donate a vehicle to The Vivian Foundation and that the dealership had, unfortunately, said no.

Joe grabbed a pen and wrote a name on a piece of paper, including the name of this person's business and their contact information. Joe assured me this individual was a God-fearing man who loved to support ministries and other community organizations.

As I sat in Joe's office, I could not help but remember the abundance of prophetic words I had received from inmates during my incarceration. I specifically remembered the words of my friend Christy who, on February 12, 2013, confidently stated, "Katie, someday someone is going to give you a Buick Enclave."

While incarcerated, I sent nightly emails to friends and family, updating them on my life and asking about theirs, to stay connected. The very same night that Christy had told me about the Buick, I sent the following email: "Guys, I'm dreaming big! Why not? As we have found out, dreams really do come true. All you need is the faith to believe. Nothing is impossible with God. Nothing!" I continually thanked God for that car despite not having its keys in my possession.

Joe slid the piece of paper across his desk, and he had written down the name of a gentleman who owned a number of car dealerships throughout the Midwest. Without mentioning anything about Christy's prophetic words, I asked him, "Does he by any chance sell Buicks?" Joe answered yes, and I felt a nudge in my spirit.

When I returned home later that day, I researched the man's name and the portfolios of the companies he owned. His organization adheres to the traditional practice of tithing, which is giving back 10 percent of its profits to the communities in which they do business. I knew God had directed my steps inside that bank, so I stepped out in faith and contacted their director of operations. I also forwarded information on *Call Me Vivian* and The Vivian

Foundation and promised his assistant that I would drop off a book when additional copies became available.

All of these good, promising things were the result of a simple trip to the bank. Then it became a matter of awaiting the manifest workings of God brought about by this meeting with Joe and the prophetic words spoken three years earlier. "The LORD directs the steps of the godly. He delights in every detail of their lives" (Psalm 37:23).

After my bank visit, I hit a couple of thrift stores to see what I could find for my family's new Christmas Eve tradition of exchanging "white elephant" gifts. These gifts often are silly, weird, or interesting, but they can also be simple and practical. Nothing grabbed my attention at the Salvation Army, so I headed across town to Goodwill. Tucked away on the shelf was a brand-new copy of *Who Moved My Cheese?* by Spencer Johnson, MD. I had already read the book, but just a few days earlier, a friend had mentioned it in conversation, so I knew God was up to something. It wasn't the perfect white elephant gift, but I headed toward the checkout counter with the book in hand.

A woman stood behind me in line and took note of the book, asking me what it was about. I told her what I remembered and then opened the front cover, which read,

> *Who Moved My Cheese?* is a simple parable that reveals profound truths. It is an amusing and enlightening story of four characters who live in a maze and look for cheese to nourish them and make them happy.
>
> Cheese is a metaphor for what you want to have in life—whether it is a good job, a loving relationship, money or a possession, health or spiritual peace of mind.
>
> And the maze is where you look for what you want—the organization you work in, or the family or community you live in.

This profound book from bestselling author, Dr. Spencer Johnson, will show you how to:

- Anticipate change
- Adapt to change quickly
- Enjoy change
- Be ready to change quickly, again and again

Discover the secret for yourself and learn how to deal with change, so that you suffer less stress and enjoy more success in your work and in life.[1]

The woman then revealed that she belonged to a book club, and I wondered if that was why God guided us to the same checkout lane. I mentioned how I had recently written a book about my spiritual journey, to which she quickly responded, "Before you say anymore, you need to know that I'm an agnostic."

That was all she had to say for me to know that, once again, I was right where I was supposed to be. I waited for her to pay for her items, and then we introduced ourselves. Her name was Betsy. We ventured toward the parking lot together and continued to chat. It turned out that we had both grown up Catholic. I explained to Betsy why I had walked away from church and how it proved to be a poor decision. I shared what the Holy Spirit placed on my heart, and Betsy seemed intrigued by my story. I promised her that I'd give her my book in two weeks, when I received extra copies, and we exchanged contact information.

According to Merriam-Webster Dictionary, the simple definition of *agnostic* is a person who does not have a definitive belief about whether God exists.[2] They're unsure. I wondered why Betsy felt that way. Although we only visited for roughly ten minutes, she, too, had shared what was on her heart. Her daughter battled childhood leukemia, so both Betsy and her daughter were in and out of hospitals for four years. It was, understandably, a terribly difficult season for them. Deeply embedded in Betsy's heart and mind were memories of other children suffering with terminal illnesses. The somberness of her tone led me to expect Betsy to conclude her story by telling me that her daughter passed away, so imagine my surprise when she told me her daughter was now in her mid-thirties. Over thirty years had passed, but Betsy still actively agonized over this experience.

In addition to struggling with her daughter's childhood leukemia, Betsy continued to suffer medical complications from metal implanted within her body after a drunk driver hit her. Every day, Betsy's chronic pain reminded her of that event. She couldn't make sense as to why God would let bad things happen. Her husband attended church, Betsy explained, and she herself was a dedicated volunteer in the community, but when it came to life beyond this world, she just wasn't sure what to think. We talked for another few minutes before she had to go, and she said, "You could preach to me all afternoon."

Betsy was right; I truly enjoy sharing my testimony and my love for the Lord, but she was not quite ready to hear what I had to say. I could sense that Betsy still suffered from these trials. Unfortunately, bad things happen to good people sometimes, and they often assign God the blame. It's tough to forgive the people who hurt us. In my spirit I knew one thing was certain: God was preparing to move Betsy's cheese, and I was going to help him.

Just before the holidays, I came across a scrap of paper from when I was in prison and couldn't help but laugh. It was a list that two of my friends and fellow inmates, Erika and Christy, had compiled of our most memorable nicknames: Chiquita, The Dragon, Garlic Bread, and Clydesdale to name a few. You see, the people in prison administration refer to prisoners by their last names, but inmates typically call each other by nicknames. In many cases, I never learned the legal names of my fellow prisoners.

With a smile on my face, I sent Erika and Christy, who left prison long before I did, an email wishing them a happy New

Year and affectionately signed my greeting with the twenty or so nicknames they had given me. Some were hilarious, while others admittedly required censorship. Needless to say, my email provided us a few laughs and helped us remember some of our happier times together. Mother Teresa may have said it best: "We shall never know all the good a simple smile can do."

What is it about laughter and smiles that are so powerful? As kids, most of us smile all the time without thinking about it, but as we grow older, our smiles and laughter diminish significantly. The average child smiles over four hundred times a day, yet the average adult smiles no more than twenty times. Kids also tend to laugh more, laughing upwards of one hundred fifty times per day while adults laugh fewer than five times each day.[3] Simply being in the presence of young children can be both entertaining and humorous.

It reminds me of one summer day when I was babysitting my grandchildren, and my grandson Colin said to me, "Grandma, I think I'm going to change my name." This wasn't something I expected to hear from a seven-year-old.

"Really, Colin? What would you like your new name to be?" I asked.

"Norm," he answered without hesitation. I couldn't stop laughing. Where had that come from?

Colin's plan to change his name got me thinking about what's in a name. Many of us go by our nicknames. For example, my birth name is Katherine; my family calls me Katie, and friends call me Kate. Of course, I had to complicate my name even further when the Lord gave me my new name: Vivian, meaning "alive, lively, or vibrant" in Latin. One of my favorite verses in the Bible is about names and can be found in Isaiah 43:1: "I have called you by name, and you are mine" (TPT).

Many recognizable characters in the Old Testament received name changes too. In the book of Genesis, God changed Abram's name to Abraham (Genesis 17:5), meaning "father of many nations"; his wife's name changed from Sarai to Sarah because she was to become the mother of many nations (Genesis 17:15), and Jacob's name changed to Israel (Genesis 32:28) because he eventually wrestled a divine angel. And in the New Testament, let us not forget about Saul (Acts 9), who later became the apostle Paul, writing several encouraging letters to believers and the church at large while imprisoned. Remember Andrew, who brought his brother Simon to meet Jesus? Jesus looked at Simon and said, "Your name is Simon, son of John—but you will be called Cephas," which translates to Peter (John 1:42). At that time, Peter had no idea that he would help build Jesus' church.

God chose new names for people in order to establish the new identities he wanted them to embody. In other words, their new names represented their new roles, some of which were special positions of leadership. Renaming people was God's way of inviting them to participate in his divine plan. It also further assured them that they and their contributions to the kingdom would fulfill God's plan.

As I reflected on my life, I was amazed at how God managed to fit all of the pieces together in order for his perfect plan to play out for me. For example, once I learned I would be going to prison, I spent more than twenty-four hours in a dental chair over the span of one week in order to have an extraordinary amount of work done. A few root canals and crowns later, my teeth looked and felt great, and I truly considered it a blessing. You see, when you're incarcerated, your ongoing is prayer is, "Lord, please do not allow me to get sick." Prison dental and medical care is substandard, and their answer to a toothache is often extraction.

During the two years I spent at Coleman Federal Correctional Complex, I experienced occasional pain in my mouth. The pain would flare up and come and go, and although it never got so bad that I worried, I knew something needed attention. After my release in January of 2014, I continued to experience occasional discomfort throughout that entire year, so I eventually made a dental appointment. It turned out that I had an infected tooth, but it was a tooth for which I had already had a root canal! I wondered, *How could that be?* The dentist explained that I was one of the less than one percent of the population who has four canals in a tooth rather than three and that it was easy for a dentist to overlook the fourth.

Since I did not have dental insurance, I stressed over how I would scrape together the money for this bill. My dentist recommended an endodontic clinic that had offices in my hometown of Racine and in two nearby cities. I called the Racine office to make an appointment and asked if it was possible to have the work done before Christmas, which was coming up soon. I could not get an appointment in Racine, but the office assistant said they may be able to schedule me at one of their other locations. I chose their Kenosha office since it was closer to my home and scheduled an appointment for the following week.

When the time of my appointment came, I pushed open the doors of the dental office in Kenosha, not knowing that God had me right where he wanted. A nurse showed me into a room, where I waited roughly five minutes before Dr. Kreutzer stepped in. He apologized for the delay, extended his hand, and introduced himself, "Hi, I'm Jim."

"Hi, Jim. I'm Katie."

He pulled up a stool, crossed his arms, and struck up a conversation: "So what do you do for a living?"

"I'm retired," I said before adding, "and I just finished writing a book."

"What kind of book?" he asked.

"A book about my spiritual journey." I wasn't sure why, but this conversation felt more like an interrogation.

"What kind of spiritual journey?"

Oh geez, I thought. *How do I answer this one?* I started, "Did you hear about the Milt Morris investigation at SC Johnson by any chance?"

"I know Milt Morris from the Kenosha Country Club," he replied.

"Well," I sheepishly admitted, "I was his girlfriend."

I now had a captive audience of one and proceeded to reveal what transpired, including a little bit about my spiritual journey.

"I need to give you one of my business cards," he said once I had finished sharing. "I own a company called Wind Chill Media Group. I buy book rights and turn them into movies."

He asked if I had signed a book contract, and I nearly fell out of the leather dental chair. I told him a publishing company had expressed interest, but I hadn't signed anything. He then explained that in a publishing contract, one sentence concerns movie rights, and he stressed the importance that I own these rights. His experience was that it was much easier to bring a movie to market by working directly with the author rather than working with the publishing company.

Are you kidding me, Lord? I thought. The odds seemed impossible that I would not only need a second root canal on a particular tooth but also find myself in the chair of an endodontist who owned a film production company. Only God could have orchestrated it so perfectly!

The coincidences piled up. I had started writing what would later become *Call Me Vivian* in February of 2009, a mere month after pleading guilty. I figured writing would be a positive, healthy way to work through my personal issues and commit my thoughts to paper. At the time, my younger sister, Susie, was a freelance writer crafting stories for local newspapers and magazines. "Would you take a look at this particular story and tell me what you think?" I innocently asked her. Susie was more than willing to help even though she was battling breast cancer at the time. Looking back, I think my writing and her editing helped distract both of us from the challenges we were facing in our respective lives.

A short time later, Susie returned my story with her revisions, and I was amazed with what she had done. For the first time I understood that my writing was not just personally therapeutic; it also had greater potential, and I knew with certainty that we would one day see my book published.

Truthfully, my writing became sporadic after that. It ebbed and flowed with my emotions. But in October of 2011, God commanded me to write the book, and I took it a little more seriously. By June of 2014, six months after my release from prison, I had completed a fair amount of writing and decided it was time to get my butt back to church.

It was an easy decision to return to Living Light Christian Church in Racine. I always felt filled with the presence of God at Living Light and routinely received a fresh anointing. I opened the glass-paned doors and climbed a dozen steps to reach the carpeted lobby, where I met a church elder named Jerry, whom I had known for years. He had been a runner since high school and was even coached in cross country as a teenager by my former husband. Jerry welcomed me home to Living Light with a giant hug. He didn't know I had finished my prison time. Few people did.

The transition from prison to home had proved more difficult for me than I anticipated. Seeing people and going places felt uncomfortable. I honestly didn't feel pulled by the Holy Spirit to return to church either. But something about that Sunday in June felt right, and I was happy to be back.

Jerry and I now shared something in common: We both had criminal records. Jerry had found himself in trouble with the law many years before and subsequently spent three years in jail shortly after graduating high school. His story of redemption is an inspiration. Upon his release, he turned his life around, earned a college degree, got married, and opened a Christian bookstore. His storefront business became increasingly successful, so he expanded his business online.

"Hey, Katie, guess what?" Jerry asked. "I started a publishing company in January."

I stood in front of him, shaking my head in disbelief. Our conversation continued, and Jerry and his wife invited me to dinner.

Everything fell into place after that. Jerry was not the primary decision-maker at the publishing company, so he explained that I would have to prove my potential in order to become a BroadStreet Publishing author. In less than a year, that door opened, and I received an offer for a book contract, which I signed on Mother's Day of 2015. The launch date of *Call Me Vivian* was set for February 1, 2016. With a release date looming, it was time to turn my dream of helping inmates and their children into a reality by securing approval for my nonprofit, The Vivian Foundation.

Establishing a nonprofit is a cumbersome process that requires strict adherence to countless state and federal requirements. In short, it's a lot of paperwork, so I chose to work with a firm called Multiplying Talents that had experience in starting nonprofits. The consensus among my nonprofit-starting acquaintances was that it would take months or possibly even years for The Vivian Foundation to receive its 501(c)(3) authorization, establishing it as a charitable organization exempt from federal income tax. Not to mention the filing fee was $900, which I did not have. Nevertheless, I trusted God and his perfect timing. I also trusted the prophetic words spoken by my grandson Nicholas when he said, "One of these days, something crazy will happen, and you'll win a bunch of money, or you'll get a bunch of time and won't have problems with your foundation. You'll be able to set it up easily."

Without my even asking her, my friend Patrice wrote a check to me for $900. The Lord had put it on her heart to gift the amount I needed to complete the task of establishing The Vivian Foundation. As Philippians 4:19 reads, "This same God who takes care of me will supply all your needs from his glorious riches, which have been given to us in Christ Jesus."

The team at Multiplying Talents, specifically Aretha Simons, who wrote all of the by-laws and managed all of the paperwork, submitted the paperwork on May 15, 2015. Thirteen days later, The Vivian Foundation received 501(c)(3) approval from the federal government. With divine intervention, The Vivian Foundation came into existence on May 28, 2015. Is anything too difficult for the Lord?

The Racine Journal Times interviewed me about my book in mid-January of 2016, and the article was set to print in the Sunday newspaper on the last day of the month. I woke up early that morning and was shocked when I could not find an article on the book anywhere in the paper. I had told several people about it, so I was not surprised when texts, inquiries, and emails started coming in, asking about its absence. My friend Julie texted me her best guess as to why the article did not appear: "Editor still tweaking and they will run Monday on a slow news day to get better placement… front page…LOL." Jerry asked me about the missing article later that morning at church. I told him I had no clue but shared with him Julie's best guess. Jerry dismissed it and supplied at least three reasons as to why the front page was not likely to happen, but in my heart, I knew that nothing was impossible with God.

Later that day, I received a phone call from the reporter at *The Racine Journal Times*. The gentleman asked me a few more questions and explained that the story would now run on Monday, the book's release date, and on none other than page 1A. After having previously received bashings on the front page of newspapers more times than I cared to remember, I had come full circle. The article, "Baptism by Fire," demonstrated how God can transform your heart and use your past to prepare you for your future. What the reporter didn't know was that Monday, February 1 was also my born-again birthday.

Sadly, it did not take long for the hurtful, judgmental comments and blogs to pop up in response. But God quickly took me to a relevant Scripture: "If you are insulted because you bear the name of Christ, you will be blessed, for the glorious Spirit of God rests upon you" (1 Peter 4:14). That verse then took me to Matthew 5:10–12.

God blesses those who are persecuted for doing right, for the Kingdom of Heaven is theirs. "God blesses you when people mock you and persecute you and lie about you and say all sorts of evil things against you because you are my followers. Be happy about it! Be very glad! For a great reward awaits you in heaven. And remember, the ancient prophets were persecuted in the same way."

Jesus said to be happy when we are persecuted for our faith. It's uncomfortable, but it takes our eyes off earthly rewards and strips away superficial belief, strengthening the faith of those of us who endure. Persecution is also an opportunity for us to set an example for others on how to maintain a kingdom mindset in the face of harassment, pressure, and offense. Members of Jesus' own family rejected him, and he endured the shame of his hometown too. That truth helped me realize that the persecution I was enduring put me in pretty good company.

On that same day of the article's release, I received prophetic words from Carol, a friend of mine from Coleman. "Katie," she said, "you will move powerfully into the glory of the Holy Spirit as you reach out to others with your story. Do not hesitate but allow God to work through you. Step out and follow Christ. Pray about everything. I know you have your little group of friends that underpin you with prayer and love. They are your haven. Use them to lay down protective prayer and to unleash the power of the Holy Spirit on your work."

Carol then prayed for me, "I pray this day, Katie, that you are clothed in Christ's righteousness. May his glory shine through you to all who stand around you. When you speak or are spoken to, the words will come from the Holy Spirit. Father, build an impregnable wall around Katie, that all arrows thrown at her will fall and not pierce her. Thank you, Lord, that you are raising up women to be your voice in these end times. May we all go forth until the end. Amen and Shalom." God indeed calls us to repent for the end of times.

That is why the LORD says,
　"Turn to me now, while there is time.
Give me your hearts.
　Come with fasting, weeping, and mourning.
Don't tear your clothing in your grief,
　but tear your hearts instead."
Return to the LORD your God,
　for he is merciful and compassionate,
slow to get angry and filled with unfailing love.
　He is eager to relent and not punish. (Joel 2:12–13)

The Bible also shares with us in the second chapter of Joel the promise of the Lord's Spirit: "I will pour out my Spirit upon all people. Your sons and daughters will prophesy. Your old men will dream dreams, and your young men will see visions. In those days I will pour out my Spirit even on servants—men and women alike" (Joel 2:28–29). The book of Joel assures us that *everyone* who calls on the name of the Lord will be saved.

When I woke the next morning on February 2, I heard in my spirit, *You are my child in whom I am well pleased!* My first radio interview was scheduled to air that day on a station located in Washington, DC. Christy lived in the DC area, so I alerted her about the broadcast. Again, she was one of my best friends in prison, and since I reached out to her about the radio interview, I couldn't help but think back on our time together in the kitchen at Coleman.

Christy worked the dish room, and I was assigned to the serving line. We were both part of the kitchen staff for lunch and dinner, but I had not spent much time with the three ladies in the dish room. In July of 2012 though, a dishwashing position opened up, and I immediately volunteered. My prayer was that the dish room would serve as my escape from the drama of the serving line. In addition to bossiness, rudeness, and the demands of a select few, it seemed as though everyone in the serving line wanted to be in charge. Deep down, I knew that all of my coworkers and even the women I served daily did their best to cope, but the frustrations of incarceration always manifested themselves in the cafeteria.

The dish room proved to be a wonderful change indeed. My impression of the dish ladies was accurate: They worked hard, avoided drama, and liked to have fun. God quickly made it clear to me, however, that Christy was my true purpose for moving to the dish room.

For the first few weeks, Christy and I got to know one another slowly, sharing a few stories about our families and how we found ourselves in prison. She couldn't help but laugh when I told her how I ended up in Coleman; she had similarly gotten caught up in fraudulent activity with the family business and received a fifteen-month sentence while her father and brother each served eighteen months in federal prison.

Christy was a real character. For most of her life, she aspired to be a baton-twirling drum majorette, so she would march around the kitchen, twirling our small, yellow-handled broom. Her spontaneity was one of the reasons I loved working with her, and she always kept me laughing. We once threw bologna at the wall to see if it would stick (it did!). And on more than one occasion, she made me laugh so hard that I wet my pants and had to return to my cell to change my clothes.

Because we started to spend so much time together, it did not take long for the two of us to open up about our lives more deeply. We developed trust and mutual respect. Maybe it was our shared sense of humor or the fact that we were so similar that we were able to talk openly about our relationships without feeling judged. It turned out that we shared a lot in common. Like me, Christy had a track record for looking for love in all the wrong places and found herself in a codependent, inappropriate sexual relationship with a married man. Like me, Christy was sure this man was her soul mate. And like me, Christy knew this relationship needed to end.

When the time felt right, I shared my testimony with Christy, who had no clue that my job change to the dish room was the result of divine intervention. I was convinced that if I managed to change her thinking and help her come to the mind of Christ in the matter, then she would eventually make God-honoring decisions in her relationships. By leveraging God's Word, I hoped that she would come to believe God's promises. It would take time, but I was certain that God directed my steps to Christy to help her see the truth.

We spent days sitting outside on the metal bleachers, working on our tans, and having heart-to-heart discussions about the men in our lives. But the Holy Spirit prompted me to share something with Christy that I knew he intended for both of us: "Don't settle for anything less than God's best." At that point, she was soul-searching and trying to establish a new direction for her life, and we both understood that we had settled for far less than God's best when it came to our former love interests.

After the radio interview aired, Christy and I exchanged a few text messages. She and her family said they found my interview quite inspiring and that it was nice to hear my voice. Christy went on to say, "You were actually my saving grace at Coleman and my reason for changing my ways. I am changed from our relationship and will forever cherish it." That made two of us.

More people started reaching out to me after reading *Call Me Vivian*, and most of them appreciated my transparency and willingness to share my story.

> I so enjoyed reading about your relationship with God and the work of the Holy Spirit in your life…I was sad when the book ended because I know your story has not. It left me wondering if you would do more writing and sharing of how God continues to use you. I know I would love to hear more…Most of all I want to thank you for sharing your story. It has stirred and renewed a great desire for more of God and his Spirit in me.

I also received a letter from an inmate at Coleman. As she read the book's final pages, a woman who had lived across the hall from me during my incarceration handed her a note that read, "Give us courage, Father, to make and live by choices that show the difference that the love of Jesus makes in our lives. Help us not to trade away eternal values for convenience and comfort." And finally, I received an email from a woman at *The 700 Club*, which read:

I believe you are only beginning to see the plan of God's redemption in your life, Katie. You don't come to Jesus by way of such a bumpy road as yours and God not have *big* plans to multiply that breaking process many times over. I view how God multiplies the work he does in one life into the lives of many as a spiritual representation of the breaking of the fish and loaves on the day he fed thousands with one little boy's lunch. Your "lunch" is going to feed, bless, save, and deliver *so* many others in the days, months, and years to come—and in many facets.

2

I felt God's words resonating deeply within me one day when I heard, *Ready or not, here I come.* Just one day later, February 9, 2016, to be exact, I received a text from Dale, a former inmate at Coleman whom God had used many times to give me heavenly direction. Her message was brief yet powerful: "You will have another child in your path. Special needs." She signed her message, "Hands and feet of Jesus." I hadn't a doubt in my mind that God was moving.

Much to my surprise, I received a phone call from Dale later that evening. The Holy Spirit was once again speaking to her, and Dale felt compelled to call and share what God had been impressing upon her heart. She told me that I was to "be open" and "think outside of the box" because another "pearl" was coming my way.

"This child is coming soon," Dale said. She sensed that this person would feel misunderstood and alone about what they had been going through. "Because of what you have experienced," she continued, "You will understand this child."

Dale did not think the special needs description would necessarily mean a physical or mental handicap. Past experiences taught me not to interpret messages from the Lord literally. Instead, I would be open to whatever God had planned for me.

The funny thing is that two weeks prior to Dale's text message and call, pearls had been at the center of a dream I had. I stood inside of a large room when a big, burly lumberjack appeared carrying a burlap bag. Mustering the strength to lift the bag over his head, he dumped out thousands of oysters onto the floor and said to me, "You need to clean them one by one." And back in 2012, while I was still incarcerated, Dale told me that God revealed to her that I was his "pearl" and that he had been refining and polishing me for the last eight years. I wept to her as I confessed that at least a dozen times while walking the outdoor track at Coleman, I would kick the gravel around and think, *Someday I am going to find a pearl here.*

After Dale called me with this word from the Lord, I knew in my heart that God's perfect plan was beginning to unfold. I reread the parable of the pearl in Matthew: "The Kingdom of Heaven is like a merchant on the lookout for choice pearls. When he discovered a pearl of great value, he sold everything he owned and bought it!" (13:45–46). In this parable, the kingdom of heaven is not the precious pearl but the merchant. Just like a merchant sells his belongings to purchase a pearl of great value, God paid the ultimate price for us through the death of his only Son. In awe of his sacrifice, I prayed a simple prayer that evening: *Lord, I'm ready. Give me the strength and courage to help this individual and to bring healing to their heart in the mighty name of Jesus.*

Just one day after talking to Dale, I woke up early and was sipping a hot cup of coffee when my phone rang. It was the gentleman whom Joe from the bank had told me about. He was calling from one of his car dealerships and told me had been reading *Call Me Vivian*. We talked briefly about why I had reached out to his company, and he told me he would pray about a vehicle for our foundation and let God direct his steps. I thanked him and told him that was all I could ask.

For years, I had been praying and believing that God would provide a car for The Vivian Foundation, and I had been thanking God for that vehicle since February of 2013 when Christy had first spoken those prophetic words that I would one day receive a Buick Enclave. About an hour after speaking to the man, I received a text message from him asking if I was able to meet that afternoon. He confirmed his location, and the distance to his dealership would require a fair amount of driving time. I quickly changed out of my sweats and hopped into my car. As I cruised down the expressway, I wondered what God had in store for me but knew one thing: God's blessings always manifested themselves at the perfect time.

I arrived at the dealership early and sat in the lobby. The owner emerged about ten minutes later, introduced himself, and led me to his office. The owner and I exchanged some small talk and basic information about ourselves, and I explained the details of God's divine intervention that led me to the chair in his office. Then he started to open up about his own life, revealing intimate details about his personal struggles. This God-fearing, successful business-man and well-respected member of his community had fallen off the path of righteousness and become ensnared in an extramarital affair that he had been trying to end.

"Your book was the final straw," he said. "It was like reading my own story. I cried like a baby and even threw your book against the wall twice, knowing that God's hand was all over this and that things needed to change."

It took me a few minutes to realize that this man seated directly across the desk from me was the special needs child that Dale had prophesied to me. We discussed the similarities of our situations, and at that moment, I truly was the only person who could relate to him. I offered insight from a woman's perspective, discussing matters he had not considered. I was brutally honest about my infidelity and the toll it had taken on my family.

He unloaded his heartache and pain for the next ninety minutes. We spoke about his wife, who was aware of the affair, and the hurt he had caused her. We spoke of repenting, seeking forgiveness, and walking in step with the Holy Spirit, whose presence in that office was undeniable. He struggled with the truth of his hypocritical behavior and how he had let so many people down. The truth was that my new friend was engaged a spiritual battle, and the devil was throwing every tactic his way in an attempt to hold him in bondage.

I felt God speaking through me when I told him, "The reason it feels like there is a dagger in your heart is because there is. Satan placed it there. It is time to remove it and let your heart heal. This is the time to take your family by the hand. Your decision to walk in obedience will have an impact on generations to come. Break the curse once and for all. It's time to start over. Your decision and next steps will have eternal consequences."

My testimony was raw and real; it was not the time to hold back. I shared things that I never thought I would disclose to another human soul, let alone someone I had met only earlier that day. Nevertheless, I knew with certainty that the Lord had called me to share the truth of my situation. The sooner we release our secrets and choose to be open and honest with ourselves and others, the sooner things change.

As I had written in *Call Me Vivian*, the two most difficult sins to resist and overcome are those of pride and sexually immorality. Pride tells us, "I deserve it," and sexual enticement says, "I need it." When combined, their appeal is deadly. Pride appeals to an empty head and sexual desire to an empty heart. However, I understand that I am living proof that with God's help and transformative power, a person can break free from the chains of sexual codependency and move forward to help others achieve that same freedom.

After almost two hours, I sensed our conversation coming to a close. We were both emotionally and spiritually exhausted. He assured me that his life would change and thanked me for stepping out in faith to publish my book. I gathered my personal items, and God's perfect timing had arrived. The dealership owner stood up, extended his right hand, and placed a key in mine. "I had to see if you were the real deal," he said. "Drive it home. We'll take care of selling your car."

Just as God had promised, I received a new Buick Encore for The Vivian Foundation. I did not know if I should laugh or cry. The car seemed so insignificant at that moment because I was truly celebrating God's work in both of our lives. It wasn't a Buick Enclave as Christy had predicted, but I believe that as an "encore," God will one day send me an Enclave.

As I drove the new car home, I promised myself that I would continue to "keep an open mind" and "think outside of the box" as Dale had suggested. Whatever was coming my way was sure to be one wild ride with God behind the wheel. Anything could happen.

Two days later, I conducted my first live radio interview with station KAYT out of Alexandria, Louisiana. I expected the interview to last roughly fifteen minutes, but time went on as the questions became increasingly personal. *If God wants me to get personal,* I thought, *then that's what God's gonna get from me.* The interview ended up lasting forty-five minutes instead of fifteen, and the same experience unfolded when I appeared on the podcast *The Debbie Chavez Show a few days later.* After the interview with KAYT, I snapped a few photos of my new car to share the good news with family and friends. As I took a closer look, I noticed the vehicle license plate contained the numbers 255, and of course the Lord encouraged me to open my Bible.

In the book of Jeremiah, the message read: "Turn from the evil road you are traveling and from the evil things you are doing. Only then will I let you live in this land that the LORD gave to you and your ancestors forever" (25:5). Jeremiah, a prophet, spoke these words, and the purpose of his book in the Old Testament is to encourage God's people to turn away from their sins and toward God. Jeremiah delivered and preached this message for twenty-three years!

God did not give up on the people of Judah, just as he does not give up on us. Even when we stumble, he never stops loving us. But we must repent. *Repent* means "to turn from sin and dedicate oneself to the amendment of one's life,"[4] and when we are willing to do that, God welcomes us with open arms. He *wants* to pour out his covenant blessings on us, but we must be willing to walk in obedience. We can find evidence of this promise in the Bible.

> If you fully obey the LORD your God and carefully keep
> all of his commands that I am giving you today, the LORD
> your God will set you high above the nations of the world.
> You will experience all these blessings if you obey the LORD
> your God: Your towns and your fields will be blessed. Your
> children and your crops will be blessed. The offspring of
> your herds and flocks will be blessed. Your fruit baskets and
> breadboards will be blessed. Wherever you go and what-
> ever you do, you will be blessed. (Deuteronomy 28:1–6)

I felt like living proof that God is, indeed, one who keeps his
word. He opened the door for me to publish my book, provided
money to start The Vivian Foundation, helped secure our nonprofit
status in record time, and supplied a new vehicle for me.

Weeks later, the time arrived for my much-anticipated lunch
date with Betsy, the woman I met in line at Goodwill.

"I loved, loved, loved your book!" she exclaimed.

We visited for nearly three hours. Betsy asked about my past
and was particularly interested in my prison experience, and I was
brutally honest with her. She was learning about a side of life that
she knew nothing about. According to the Prison Policy Initiative,
"The American criminal justice system holds almost 2.3 million
people in 1,833 state prisons, 110 federal prisons, 1,772 juvenile
correctional facilities, [and] 3,134 local jails…There are another
840,000 people on parole and a staggering 3.6 million people on
probation."[5] Anyone would find these numbers shocking, yet the
prison system and incarcerated life remain a mystery to most.

I told Betsy how my prison ministry work began the day that
I walked into Coleman, and a lot of the time, that meant lending
an ear to women who needed to unload their heartache and pain.
One inmate admitted she had been in the wilderness for forty
years because of domestic violence. Another was having an affair
and didn't have the strength to end it. An older woman nicknamed
Grandma faced a sentence of four months but knew it would lead

to the spiritual growth of her family. One woman struggled with codependency and could not seem to keep out of trouble, and another woman was a drug dealer and recovering addict. I met a woman in her seventies who was writing a book and a woman who never felt loved. I found it noteworthy how God surrounded me with women who shared experiences similar to mine.

On a few occasions, God even used me as the hands and feet of Jesus to help make a difference in the lives of others. A young girl named Victoria was struggling with her incarceration and harbored anger toward God. It was tough to listen to her story, especially when she retold her childhood memories. As a kid, she lived in a shelter, and prison reminded her of that time, making her adjustment to Coleman difficult. In kindergarten, someone had sexually molested her, which explained why she was afraid to go into the prison's bathroom and shower area alone. She had been writing to help release the pain of the childhood abuse and even showed me her journal. Victoria's heart desperately needed healing, and I was able to bless her with much-needed resources and encouragement.

I also told Betsy how God had directed my steps to comfort a coworker at Coleman. This woman worked in the kitchen office, and when I arrived for work in the serving line, she appeared visibly upset. I guided her into the office where we could talk privately.

"Scheller, my grandma is very sick and dying. This is the only time I've felt like I'm in prison. There's nothing I can do."

"Yes, there is," I confidently replied. "We can pray."

I took her hands and prayed one of the most beautiful prayers I've ever prayed, asking the Holy Spirit to intervene on her behalf. Two days later, when I saw this woman on the compound, she had a big smile on her face and hugged me. Her grandmother was out of intensive care and complaining. I worried that complaining meant she was still ill.

"Katie, if she is complaining, then our prayers have been answered," she assured me. "That means she's getting back to her old self!"

And then there was Candi, who was so happy to hear her name during mail call for three nights in a row that she came by my cell to thank me and give me a hug. I had coordinated with friends on the "outside" to send cards and letters to inmates who never received mail, and the impact it had on these women was life changing. Candi came back a second time that particular evening after opening a letter from my friend, Phyllis.

"I need to tell you something," Candi continued. "My grandma was a very faith-filled person. She used to take me to church seven days a week. But then I got away from church, and I got into a lot of trouble. My grandma died two years ago, and I've been in prison for nine. Phyllis' words reminded me of my grandma, and I just needed to tell you that. Phyllis sent things to encourage me."

We were both overcome with emotion, and Candi asked if I would please thank Phyllis for her. I told her I would, and I also reminded Candi that her grandma was looking down from heaven and was pleased with the progress Candi was making at holding her tongue and cleaning up her language. A small word of encouragement, a listening ear, and a simple act of kindness can truly change a person's life: "Do not withhold good from those who deserve it when it's in your power to help them" (Proverbs 3:27).

As Betsy listened, I detailed other life-changing moments that took place during the early stages of my incarceration. On Wednesday, February 29, 2012, just two months into my sentence, a woman I had never met came through the serving line and asked me for the name of my book. I hadn't even told anyone that I was writing a book, so my first thought was, *Who is this woman, and why is she asking me this question?* Nevertheless, I sensed in my spirit that God was up to something and shared the book's title with her.

The next day, while I was serving dessert, the same woman approached me and confidently stated, "It's going to be a bestseller!"

With a smile on my face, I asked her, "Have you been talking to God?"

She returned a smile and said, "Yes, I have." If I hadn't been serving food, I might have slapped myself out of shock. I was so happy that it felt as if my feet hovered above the ground.

Later, I returned to my unit after lunch to shower. "It's going to be a bestseller!" I shouted as the hot water bounced off my head. I am convinced that the joy I felt in that moment was the exact same joy that David experienced when he danced naked in front of the Lord. I prayed in the Spirit and danced around for thirty minutes, thanking God for what he would do with *Call Me Vivian*.

On Friday, two days after our initial meeting, I saw my new friend again and asked, "Any messages today?"

"No," she said. "Nothing today."

Despite her earlier prophetic message from God about my book's future, I still did not know her name. "Who are you," I asked, "and where do you live?"

"My name is Ivory. I live in unit F3."

On Monday evening, I located Ivory and learned she was originally from Brooklyn, New York. She had been at Coleman for eighteen months, and her release was scheduled for September of 2015, which would complete her nine-year sentence. Ivory was a true worshiper who loved the Lord and had the gift "to see in the Spirit." She even said she undergirded me "like Aaron did for Moses" when Moses lacked the strength to carry on.

"Something about you stood out," Ivory said about first seeing me on the compound. She knew in her heart that we would connect.

Ivory laughed as she explained to me how I had interfered with her worship on the day that she first asked me about my book. My face kept appearing in her mind as she prayed earlier that morning. My face appeared many times before God told her to ask me for the title of my book. She admitted that she was reluctant to ask me about it at first, but because she is obedient, she did as the Lord instructed. She was relieved but not surprised to learn that I was indeed writing a book. God told her to pray for me.

The morning after Ivory had first approached me, and again while worshiping, my face appeared in her mind again: "Your face was actually becoming rather annoying," she said. But soon after, God told her to tell me that my book would become a bestseller.

I could not help but think back to January of 2009 when I pled guilty in federal court. Before the judge announced his verdict, he told me about a man he had sentenced who went on to write a successful book. As I waited for him to decide my fate, I wondered, *Why in the world is he telling this story?*

While I was getting to know my new friend, Ivory, I received in the mail a devotion written by A. J. Russell from his book *God Calling*. It contained a powerful reading entitled "Claim Big Things," which read:

> Listen, listen I am your Lord. Before Me, there is none other. Just trust me in everything. Help is here all the time. The difficult way is nearly over, but you have learned lessons you could learn in no other way. "The Kingdom of Heaven suffered violence, and it is the violent who take it by force." Wrest from Me, by firm and simple trust and persistent prayer, the treasure of My Kingdom.
>
> Such wonderful things are coming to you, Joy—Peace—Assurance—Security—Health—Happiness—Laughter. Claim big, really big things now. Remember nothing is too big. Satisfy the longing of My Heart to give.[6]

The timing of that devotion paired with Ivory's prophetic words helped fuel my passion for writing and gave me the confidence to pursue it. I would write daily summaries of what happened at Coleman and email them home to friends and family; that way, I had an archive of the experiences, events, and details of what took place for inclusion in my book.

When May of 2012 rolled around, marking four months in jail, I thought back to my time working in corporate America. It was not uncommon to give and receive performance reviews, and I imagined what kind of performance review I would receive for my time at Coleman.

The first step in any performance review is to solicit feedback. I sensed the guy upstairs wanted me to set limitations on who I might ask: *You cannot ask anyone from your Bible Study group because you know they would give you a glowing report. Ask your bunkies, your coworkers, and your neighbors.* So I did and posed the following prompt to each of them: "Tell me something about Scheller."

I was almost afraid to ask given that prison can be an environment of brutal honesty, and many inmates carried a glass-half-empty attitude. You can imagine my surprise when every woman I asked told me to focus on the positive, and they were right. Hearing their feedback made me realize that I was surrounded by women with good hearts; my heart, however, still needed work. All too often, I would focus on the qualities and behaviors in others that I disliked. God, of course, saw this in my heart as well and identified it as a growth opportunity for me. I needed to change my ways and focus on the positive qualities of every woman I met.

Our speech and our actions reveal our true underlying beliefs, attitudes, and motivations. Whatever a person chooses to treasure will determine what emerges in his or her life. As Luke 6:45 reads, "A good person produces good things from the treasury of a good heart, and an evil person produces evil things from the treasury of an evil heart. What you say flows from…your heart." Now that I understood this, I needed to put into practice Philippians 4:8: "Fix your thoughts on what is true, and honorable, and right, and pure, and lovely, and admirable. Think about things that are excellent and worthy of praise."

Once I had finished sharing these prison stories with Betsy, I could sense that she was beginning to see another side of life by spending time with me. Slowly but surely, her cheese was beginning to move. I was surprised to hear her say, "You will star as yourself in the movie about your life. Who else could play you?" Another friend had told me the same thing just two years earlier.

God was up to something, and I recalled a fun conversation in prison when I talked to my fellow inmates about a future movie about my life. I told each of them I would do my best to have them and our counselor cast in the prison portion. I asked them which celebrities they would want to play them, and their answers included actors such as Cameron Diaz and Drew Barrymore. Then I asked who they thought should play me.

"Oh, that's an easy one!" they agreed. "Betty White!"

I couldn't think of a greater compliment! Betty White was hilarious, quick-witted, and an all-around national treasure. For the record, most of my friends agree that I'm more of a Sophia when it comes to the *Golden Girls*.

Over time, the movie-themed nudges from heaven continued. During my second year of incarceration, we were given a handout called "But, Nevertheless":

You are the Actor and God is the Director. Each morning you should fire yourself, stand aside, and let God direct and guide you through daily life.

In life we are used to running so many things, yet the only thing we really run is our mouth. It is when you have matured enough that you are able to put the microphone of life down and let God run your show.

It is no wonder your show is either getting canceled or no one is watching it because you want to be the actor, producer, and director. When you finally (hopefully it will not take a lifetime) say, "But nevertheless, Lord, I want your will, not mine," you will walk the red carpet. God is saying, "Surrender your show to me and I will make it win an Academy Award."

Then, during a promotional interview for *Call Me Vivian*, a local radio station host said, "I see a movie coming!" At least fifty other people have said the same thing. Personally, I continue to bank on what my grandson, Colin, prophesized in 2014: "Your book will be a hit movie and a bestseller. It will be a good success!"

Some may call me crazy or delusional for claiming a best-selling book and award-winning film, but I claim prosperity and God's favor in everything that I do. I claim no weapon formed against me will prosper, and I claim miracle after miracle in the mighty name of Jesus. I have given away ten times more copies of *Call Me Vivian* than I have sold. I can't help but laugh because I'm aware of how that sounds, but I stand firmly on the promises found in God's Word: "God is not a man, so he does not lie. He is not human, so he does not change his mind. Has he ever spoken and failed to act? Has he ever promised and not carried through?" (Numbers 23:19).

In March of 2016, my friend Kathie received a "download" from heaven about my journey and emailed it to me. It was much longer than this, but I've chosen a few selections that particularly stand out:

"To me, you are very dear, and I love you" (Isaiah 43:4 CEV)...How delighted I AM with your tenacity. Like a pup with a bone, you would not let go or be denied in doing what I called you to do. Whatever stood in your way, your passionate desire to serve and obey allowed you to persevere. True to the calling on your life, you continue to reveal my heart, share love's fire, and extend my invitation to intimacy. And for a time such as this, I've called and prepared you and others like you to revive, refresh, and restore. Empowered to proclaim and witness the miraculous. "I want you woven into a tapestry of love, in touch with everything there is to know of God" (Colossians 2:2 MSG). "Be an example to all believers in what you say, in the way you live, in your love, your faith, and your purity" (1 Timothy 4:12). Whatever still lingers and hinders you from your past... the time has come to let go of those things that won't last.

Then in late July, some months after Kathie's email, my family attended the Huntington's Disease Society of America (HDSA) walk/run fundraiser. My son, Brian, and his wife, Ellie, have been actively involved in the Wisconsin chapter of HDSA. For those who may not be familiar with Huntington's disease, it is a rare, inherited genetic disorder that leads to a progressive breakdown of nerve cells in the brain. The good news is that scientists have made great advancements in Huntington's disease research, which gives us hope. In fact, the name of the fundraiser that year was "Team Hope," and the money raised would be donated to help support research efforts to find a cure.

The organization planned a two-mile walk (or run) around a local high school track, a silent auction, and a 50/50 raffle in which half of the money paid to purchase a raffle ticket goes to the organization and the other half goes toward a prize awarded to someone at the end of the event. The organizers sold a ton of tickets that day. Someone was going home with a healthy amount of cash!

With temperatures in the nineties and dew points hovering near seventy degrees, there was only one thing to do that day: sweat. The countdown for the race wound down, and the blow horn sounded. Hundreds of participants began their two-mile trek. Given the heat, it wasn't surprising that only a few participants chose to run, yet one little boy, who was not more than ten years old, ran and finished in second place. After he crossed the finish line, he met the cheering crowd with a huge smile on his face. When I saw him afterward, I noticed that his shoes were literally falling off his feet. All ten of his toes were visible, and I wasn't sure if that was from wear-and-tear or if he had simply outgrown them. Then I observed his large family. A number of children were in tow, and they appeared poor in terms of material items.

The anticipation grew among the crowd until it was finally time for the 50/50 raffle drawing. The announcer gave the six-digit sequence over the loudspeaker. Everyone scrambled to read their tickets, hoping to find the winning combination in their hand.

Then a woman's voice cried out, "We won!" She held her ticket in the air, triumphant. Wouldn't you know it (and I believe it was a little bit of divine intervention), the family of the little boy won the grand prize. Again, the little boy beamed. His smile was infectious; I, too, smiled at the gift that God bestowed upon them.

Despite the family's obvious financial needs and their son's desperate need for a new pair of shoes, they immediately returned the prize money to HDSA. Though they might have lacked in finances, they were certainly blessed with richness in their hearts. Their kindness brought me to tears. It was an unforgettable lesson in sacrificial giving not only for me but also for everyone who witnessed this family's selfless act of generosity. Generosity is a god-like quality. It benefits everyone, and God loves a cheerful giver. Jesus teaches about giving in the Bible.

> Jesus sat down near the collection box in the Temple and watched as the crowds dropped in their money. Many rich people put in large amounts. Then a poor widow came and dropped in two small coins. Jesus called his disciples to him and said, "I tell you the truth, this poor widow has given more than all the others who are making contributions. For they gave a tiny part of their surplus, but she, poor as she is, has given everything she had to live on." (Mark 12:41–44)

The widow was doing exactly what Jesus had told the rich, young ruler to do: "Go and sell your possessions and give the money to the poor, and you will have treasure in heaven. Then come, follow me" (Mark 10:21).

Jesus went on to explain why it is difficult for the rich to enter the kingdom of God. The rich, having their basic physical needs met, often become self-reliant. Whenever they feel empty, they buy something new in an attempt to fill the void that only God can fill. Their abundance and self-sufficiency become their deficiency. The person who has everything on earth can still lack what is most important: eternal life.

It was at that point that God moved my heart and told me to bless that little guy with my shoes. Not only were the shoes on my feet a brand-new pair in an appropriate color for a boy, but when I asked him to come near my seat and try them on, they also turned out to be a perfect fit. I told him he could have them, and then he ran back to his mom to show her. She thanked me from a distance with a smile and a wave. As I walked toward my car, socks and all, my sister asked, "Where are your shoes?" I smiled and knew that I had just sown into this young man's running career.

We all need hope. Hope is the anchor of the soul. It's synonymous with optimism and courage; in fact, the Bible defines *hope* as "confident expectation" (see Zechariah 9:12). Whether I'm sharing a message of hope in prison or in a coffee shop with a new friend like Betsy, helping friends or family, or writing at home, I enjoy whatever God calls me to do. I think it's because I was a late bloomer when it came to Christianity. Unresolved childhood fears made it extremely difficult for me to find my way throughout most of my adult life. It wasn't until I was in my early fifties that I was born again. What I realized, however, was that God had been preparing my heart long before then to ensure my success, and he started in my childhood.

As a kid who loved to participate in sports, I understood competition from a young age. In order to compete and get the most out of myself, I knew that I needed confidence, leadership skills, team skills, and determination. Regardless of where life might take me, I knew this with certainty: No matter how difficult the circumstances, I would never give up. My goal has always been to do everything to the best of my ability and to have fun.

When I examine my life more objectively, I recognize that everything that happened in my life was necessary for my spiritual growth. I enjoyed a tremendous amount of pride in my achievements and possessions, and as a result, God had no choice but to empty me of all of it. I had gained the whole world but lost my soul in the process.

Since hitting rock bottom, God directed (and continues to direct!) my steps, which facilitated a miraculous change in my heart. By volunteering at nursing homes and caring for the disabled, I developed my compassion. By relying on family, friends, and strangers for support, I learned to humble myself.

One of the most important lessons God taught me was when I coached my daughter's second grade basketball team. Trust me when I tell you this role required endurance in patience. As is true of all kids and adults, some possess natural athleticism while others do not. Some of the girls did not know the first thing about basketball. Others lacked the coordination to dribble a ball or even run, and some did not have the physical strength to launch the ball up toward the basket.

With youngsters, I've found that the best approach to teaching them a new game is to stress the fundamentals. While doing that and helping them acquire new skills, we built a foundation of trust. Whether we were practicing or playing a game, I made sure we had fun. We once wore funny noses and glasses during warmups; another time it was Santa hats. I always tried to make our time enjoyable. Nevertheless, it took an entire season for many of the girls to understand what they were supposed to be doing on the court. The most precious moment, however, was when they finally made their first basket.

That's when it hit me: Jesus took some of the most unlikely players and, slowly but surely, developed them into remarkable men and women of faith. That was his coaching style. Some of his greatest stars were completely unaware of their capabilities and did not understand how God would use them on his team.

God's work requires all kinds of different people with unique gifts and abilities. There are no superstars—only team members who excel in their roles. We can all become useful members of God's team by setting aside whatever personal desires we may have to shine. Don't seek human praise; seek God's approval. And as 1 Peter 3:8 reads, we should "be of one mind. Sympathize with each other. Love each other as brother and sisters. Be tenderhearted, and keep a humble attitude." Peter lists five key elements that should characterize any team of believers:

1. Pursue the same goals.
2. Be responsive to the needs of others.
3. Treat others as brothers and sisters.
4. Be affectionately sensitive and caring.
5. Encourage one another and rejoice in each other's successes.

God has shown me so clearly that the joy of the Lord comes when you help someone who everyone else has given up on and show them that you care.

3

During the third week of May of 2016, I traveled to Atlanta for The Vivian Foundation's first event: a three-day conference hosted by the Correctional Ministries and Chaplains Association (CMCA). The mission of the CMCA is to connect, encourage, equip, and strengthen Christians as they fulfill the Great Commission in corrections. CMCA's belief is that the power of Christ can transform the lives of the incarcerated, formerly incarcerated, and their families to strengthen communities. Their goal is to support correctional ministry professionals, volunteers, and organizations as they serve those affected by crime and incarceration while ensuring public safety.[7]

Bound for Atlanta with my car packed full of ministry resources, I budgeted two days of travel time, leaving me with several hours to reflect on everything that had taken place since my release from prison. If all of it hadn't happened to me personally, I'm not sure that I would believe it. Two friends of mine from Tampa, Paula and Patrice, were to meet me in Atlanta to help me with the conference. We had talked about this event for months, and none of us knew what to expect.

Once all three of us arrived, we enjoyed a nice dinner together before returning to the hotel early. I felt exhausted from the drive and determined to get a good night's sleep. Tossing and turning in anticipation, I might have slept three hours at most. In the morning, we set up our table and hung our banners, and our display looked great. Spread across the table were marketing materials and books, ready and waiting to reach the hands of hundreds of attendees.

God's presence was powerful at the conference those next three days. The testimonies, tears, and personal stories of so many people touched our hearts and were evidence of God's infinite grace. I met former inmates, some of whom only recently obtained their release. One man, whom the court had wrongly convicted, spent more than half of his adult life behind bars before the declaration of his innocence.

There was Latoya, who approached our table and asked us for a big hug. I held her as she broke down in tears. She thanked me for starting The Vivian Foundation because she was one of "those kids"—left homeless as a result of her mother's criminal past and incarceration. She was the only family member around to raise her younger brother, and she was still grieving and processing everything she endured.

Then there was Miko, who was involved in re-entry programs in the Atlanta area. He poured out his heart in a way that I had never experienced. His vulnerability while sharing his pain and heartache was powerful. We could not help but feel touched by the love he received from his family and friends despite the struggles and challenges that life had thrown his way.

God opened another door for me that weekend. Best-selling author Carol Kent attended the conference as the keynote speaker. I'd read all of her books and always hoped to meet her, and not only did I meet her, but I also enjoyed breakfast with her and her husband, Gene. Their life was turned upside down when their only child, Jason, committed murder and was issued a life sentence in the state of Florida.

Carol and Gene are passionate about helping inmates and their families adjust to their new normal. Together, they founded the nonprofit organization Speak Up for Hope, which benefits prisoners and their families. Carol, Gene, and I discussed many aspects of their ministry work, notably how to embrace hidden gifts that can be found amid undesirable circumstances. I listened intently to Carol's words of wisdom and knew in my heart that only God could have arranged that breakfast meeting. He was teaching me through the experiences of others, and a vast amount of knowledge was transferred to me during our brief meal together. His perfect plan was unfolding right before my eyes in a way that I had only dreamed possible.

Another highlight for me was watching Voices of Hope, a choir from the Lee Arrendale Prison. Their performance touched me to the core, and they received multiple standing ovations throughout their set. I wondered about each of their stories. I wondered about their individual crimes and sentences. I wondered what thoughts crossed their minds after enjoying a glimpse of freedom and normalcy for a few hours in the outside world. My heart broke when they left the auditorium, knowing that boarding the bus to return to prison was the last thing they wanted to do.

As the weekend progressed, I met countless other men and women committed to helping inmates, former inmates, and their families. One woman's story stands out in my memory. She introduced herself as Scottie Barnes, a woman who was in her seventies and a child of an incarcerated parent. That weekend, CMCA was formally recognizing Scottie and her husband, Jack, for their tireless years of service in corrections ministry. Their personal ministry, Forgiven Ministry, was based in Taylorsville, North Carolina. It was established as a 501(c)(3) nonprofit organization in October of 2000, but its story began in 1995, when Scottie and Jack were running a thriving business in Taylorsville. Busy following their own plans and pursuits in life, Scottie admitted that she and Jack had never asked God about his plan for them.

Then one day, the chaplain of the local prison in their small town walked into their boutique and asked Scottie if she would speak at the prison's Sunday night worship service. *I never intend to go back to prison,* Scottie thought. *I visited my father behind bars since the age of four, virtually all my life.*

Scottie looked at the chaplain and said, "I really don't have anything to say."

With a sincere look on his face, the chaplain asked, "Wasn't your daddy saved before he served his last prison term as a drug kingpin?"

Scottie remembered Matthew 25:36: "I was in prison, and you visited me." Scottie agreed to visit the local prison, and when she spoke, her testimony unfolded with such an anointing that she knew she was in the presence of God doing his perfect will. She felt God calling her and Jack into ministry to help children who experienced the same type of loneliness and separation that she had.

Given the hundreds of thousands of lives that Forgiven Ministry has since touched, we are all grateful that Scottie and Jack answered God's call. Forgiven Ministry also participates in "One Day with God," the program I mentioned in the introduction that reunites children with their incarcerated parents and guides them through a series of fun, spiritual-based activities.

In addition to her ministry work, Scottie published two thirty-day devotionals called *Silent Victims* and *Hands Reaching, Hearts Touching*, both of which shine the light of God into the world of a child who, through no fault of their own, has had a parent taken away from them. Inspiration for these heartwarming books came from letters, prayers, and poems from children of incarcerated parents, inmates, caregivers, and Forgiven Ministry volunteers.

Scottie's third book, *All for Him: A Journey from Brokenness to Reconciliation*, reveals how Scottie longed for her father's love, but his rejection and emotional detachment left her heartbroken and imprisoned by feelings of anger, bitterness, and resentment. Once she accepted God's love, however, she understood that God's sacrificial gifts of grace and mercy were her greatest blessing. Her newfound joy and peace allowed her to embody compassion, humility, and forgiveness. Her father's salvation became her life's ambition even though it would take forty-one years before she would hear her dad utter the words, "I love you, Scottie."

As I listened to Scottie's story, I could not help but think of Galatians 6:9: "Don't allow yourselves to be weary in planting good seeds, for the season of reaping the wonderful harvest you've planted is coming!" (TPT). The Vivian Foundation blessed Forgiven Ministry with our "Heaven Cent" poems, "Just One Word Bible Reading Plans," and a large quantity of *Call Me Vivian* books for their women's programs. When Scottie asked if our "Heaven Cent" poems were available in Spanish, I told her, "They will be soon if that's what God is telling us we need!" A short time later, we shipped thousands of Spanish versions to Forgiven Ministry. God was beginning to open the doors through which he wanted me to walk, one with the help of an Oklahoma senator.

On one occasion, an older gentleman wearing a suit and tie paced in front of my table. With his hands clasped behind his back, I wondered what he was thinking as he studied my "Meet the Author" sign, the design of which looked like my prison identification card. It included my name, inmate number, date of birth, and date of my release. Finally, he stopped and approached my table. We chatted about my ministry and my book, and I gave him a copy of *Call Me Vivian*. As he paged through it, he asked me if I had heard of Ann Edenfield's ministry in Albuquerque called Wings for Life International. I said I had not, as this was my first conference. He then handed me his business card and suggested I contact her. He was familiar with her work and thought it would be good for us to connect.

It was becoming increasingly apparent that God was serious about all of the things he called me to do. All of these ministries were well established and successful inside of prisons throughout the United States and beyond.

After the CMCA conference, I drove to Florida. I received an invitation to speak at Coleman's annual Woman 2 Woman conference later that month, so it made sense to spend three weeks in Tampa instead of driving back to Wisconsin only to return a short while later. I planned to spend quality time with friends before returning to Coleman.

While in Tampa, a group of friends and I decided to go out for dinner one evening, and we ended up at Columbia Restaurant, Florida's oldest dining establishment, in Ybor City. Founded in 1905 by the Hernandez Gonzmart family, the fourth and fifth generations now own and operate multiple locations of Columbia Restaurant. Everyone else had eaten there before, and from our conversation, it sounded like I would be having a Cuban sandwich, a 1905 salad, or both.

It was Memorial Day weekend and busy at the restaurant, so we struggled to find a parking spot. Once we did, we wondered how long the wait for seating might be. This restaurant inhabits a full city block, boasts fifteen dining rooms, and seats 1,700 people at one time. Much to our surprise, the wait was brief.

Our server was a young man by the name of Steven. He was polite and attentive, and when it came time to pay our bill, we all decided to bless him by doubling his tip. I reached into my purse for extra cash and impulsively decided to also grab one of the cards that I use to market my book. I placed it inside the leather check presenter along with the cash.

We prepared to leave, but first I stopped by the Don Quixote room, one of the larger areas inside the building, for a peek. The room itself made you feel as if you'd stepped back in time to its grand opening in 1935. Colorful tiles covered the floor, Quixote-themed art lined the walls, warm light shined through stained-glass windows, and palm trees surrounded a mosaic-tiled fountain. I couldn't find a single empty table.

On our way out, Steven found me. "You guys are believers," he said. The Bible verse on the card must have given us away.

"Yes," I affirmed before telling him about *Call Me Vivian*, the spiritual transformation of my heart, and the two years I spent in federal prison.

Steven went on to tell us that he, too, was involved in prison ministry and that his brother was a pastor. "Well then," I told him, "This must be a divine appointment. I have a feeling I'll be seeing you again soon!"

The next day, I returned to Colombia Restaurant with books and resources from The Vivian Foundation, knowing that God would use the divine connection between Steven and me to advance his kingdom. God never ceases to amaze me with how he directs our steps and puts us exactly where we are supposed to be.

Next, I drove to Titusville to visit the Prison Book Project. Ray Hall started the Prison Book Project more than twenty-five years ago, and he and his wife, Joyce, have been instrumental in touching the lives of the incarcerated by shipping millions of Christian books into nearly three thousand jails and prisons throughout the country. Joining me on my visit was my friend Ruth Ann Nylen from Really Good News Ministries. She helped develop The Vivian Foundation's "Just One Word Bible Reading Plan" and penned the book *The Radical Power of God*. We loaded her vehicle with thousands of her books to donate to the Prison Book Project.

Upon our arrival, I opened the glass door that bore the Prison Book Project's logo and could not stop smiling. I was finally going to meet Ray and Joyce and thank the people who sent me the New Living Testament red-letter Bible during my incarceration. I had talked to them on numerous occasions after my release, as The Vivian Foundation supports their ministry. I also forwarded additional copies of my book to their warehouse with the goal of getting at least one book into each of their facilities. Since then, thousands of *Call Me Vivian* books have been shipped into US prisons.

What Ray and Joyce did not know was that we also had business to discuss. That red-letter Bible that was sent to me on behalf of the Prison Book Project was used to develop our "Just One Word Bible Reading Plan," which The Vivian Foundation launched in 2017. After sharing this news with them, I asked Ray how many Bible reading plans he thought their ministry could help us distribute.

Confidently, he replied, "Ten thousand." And just like that, ten thousand inmates would receive an introduction to the saving power of a relationship with Jesus Christ. In the end, we printed and distributed twenty-five thousand Bible reading plans.

Our hearts could not help but feel touched by the impact that one red-letter Bible had on all of us. All along, God knew how this would play out. He wanted the Prison Book Project to be involved in the distribution of our "Just One Word Bible Reading Plan." Maybe it was his way of thanking Ray and Joyce for everything their ministry does for inmates.

Ray broke down in tears as he experienced the ripple effect of his book ministry's hard work, which began in 1994. After touring a corrections facility, he saw the need to provide higher quality material than what was available in the jail library. Ray visited several churches that responded to his plea for help, which birthed the Prison Book Project. Today, with the help of Christian publishers, authors, volunteers, and generous donors, the Prison Book Project has become one of the most successful prison book ministries in the country. And we're happy to report that at least one copy of *Call Me Vivian* is in every jail and prison that the Prison Book Project supports, and hopefully, *Vivian's Call* will also become as readily available.

My time in Florida flew by, and soon I would walk back through the doors of Coleman. But this time, I was returning as a guest speaker, not an inmate. Two and a half years after my release, I had become an author, the president of a nonprofit organization, and a motivational speaker. I drove north on I-75, counting the mile markers in anticipation of reaching exit 321. I had made this trip a few times before: once on the day I surrendered and two other times when officers transported me in chains and shackles to the Tampa International Airport.

The terrain was familiar, but the emotions could not have been more different. How would I feel when I drove onto the compound? I wasn't sure. One thing I was all too aware of was that I was returning to the largest federal prison in the country to do exactly what God called me to do: inspire inmates with a message of hope.

I parked my car, and the first building to catch my attention was F4, my old unit. The inmates were expecting me, so it was not a surprise when I saw a few of them standing on the porch and waving. I unloaded the car and approached the front entrance, peering through the double doors. One of my friends stood on the grounds, and I spotted the chaplain in the visiting room. I opened the door and wheeled in a cart full of books. Much to my surprise, my arms went into the air, and I began praying in my prayer language. As strange as this sounds, the pure joy I felt in that moment was unlike anything I had ever experienced. The only feeling I can liken it to is making a game-winning shot at the sound of the buzzer. I walked the entire length of the visiting room with my arms in the air and greeted Chaplain Garcia with a big hug.

The doors opened forty-five minutes ahead of the program, and many of the inmates who knew me dropped by beforehand to say hello. I spent quality time with each of them, sharing words of wisdom and encouragement. Given that I had attended events like this before, I knew what to expect, and I knew that it was going to be a fun afternoon. My only regret was that these conferences are not video recorded; quite frankly, they should be. Trust me when I tell you that faith-based conferences and worship services in prison are unique and exciting in their own way.

The women filed into the visiting room, and I recognized another familiar face: Miss Elaine. Elaine lived in F4 with me and had been incarcerated for over twenty years. The moment our eyes met, our tears began to flow. During my two years at Coleman, I shared many books with Elaine. She was always happy to receive something new to read. She and I had a little tradition too. Elaine would not accept a book from me without first encouraging me to sign it. "You have to practice," she'd say. For her, I ended up autographing dozens of books that I had no hand in writing! Elaine closely examined *Call Me Vivian* and The Vivian Foundation banners that flanked the podium. She kept shaking her head and smiling, remembering all of the times we spoke about the book and the work that God would do.

The program lasted about two hours and included praise and worship by the Coleman Choir, corporate prayer, a performance by the Coleman Dance Team, and presentations by two other guest speakers. Both ladies spoke of their respective challenges in life and how we can overcome anything with the power and love of God.

When the time came for me to speak, I was in my element. While incarcerated, I had stepped up to that microphone on three occasions during Toastmasters meetings. Toastmasters was one of many programs offered to inmates, and I took advantage of it. Our meetings occurred on Thursday evenings, and these gatherings were always well attended. Many women wanted to develop their learning, speaking, and leadership skills, and the program allowed many of us an opportunity to speak in front of a group about our personal lives without feeling judged.

I spoke during these meetings on numerous occasions. My first speech was about what I wanted to be when I grew up. My second speech was titled "Service with a Smile," and my last message was "Get out of Jail Free!" I enjoyed researching the respective subject matter, incorporating Scripture into my speeches, and creatively delivering my messages, although I always lost points for exceeding the allotted time limit. Do you think God set a time limit on Jesus' sermons? Giving God all the glory takes more than five to seven minutes! Still, I knowingly took the hit every time because I knew that what I had to say was important.

The time had arrived for me to become a real motivational speaker in the women's prison that trained me, so I turned myself over to the Holy Spirit. Many of the women I had befriended were still serving their time, so I was able to share the lessons I had learned at Coleman while the Lord prepared my heart for my call to ministry. I shared the lesson found in Romans 4:17 to speak things that are not as if they were. Then I connected that lesson to all of the things that many of us had spoken into existence with *Call Me Vivian* and The Vivian Foundation. I reminded each of them that God has a great plan for their life, and while they are at Coleman, God's plan and purpose for them is to mend their broken hearts and prepare them for whatever is next.

"Don't ever give up hope," I stressed. "God is a God of the impossible. Romans 2:11 tells us that he has no favorites, so if he can do this for me, he can do it for you!"

The conference came to a close, and I gave each attendee a book. I signed autographs for close to thirty minutes, including one for Miss Elaine. All that practice finally paid off!

Returning to the compound was indeed special. I never realized how much the spiritual training ground of Coleman meant to me. It was my home for 740 days after all. For two years, it was where I received guidance from the Holy Spirit, which prepared me for my ministry calling. It may have been prison for the other five hundred inmates, but for me it was the place where God did his best work. It's where he transformed my heart and taught me the truth about true love. As I exited the building and returned to my car for the drive back to Wisconsin, I knew with certainty that God had made me precisely for a time such as this.

4

A few months passed after my speaking gig at Coleman, and my busy summer wound down. Personal and business matters had filled my calendar, and I had been hard at work developing new resources for The Vivian Foundation, which proved time-consuming. I had traveled to Florida in August and returned with my brother who, after more than thirty years away from home, wanted to be closer to family. We packed up everything he owned, rented a U-Haul, and spent two days driving back to Racine. Throw in the normal activities of life along with a daily exercise regimen, and I was exhausted.

When September arrived, I visited Minnesota to see my grandkids and attend a few of their upcoming cross country meets. I was supposed to be in Milwaukee for a scheduled, televised interview with CBS, but I suggested they feature another ministry called Faith, Hope, and Love, which supports foster children as well as children of incarcerated parents. The Vivian Foundation supports their ministry, and the timing was perfect for them since it coincided with their fall event. I couldn't wait to spend quality time with my son and grandkids and enjoy some much-needed rest.

A few days after arriving in Minnesota, the Lord prompted me to visit Carver Park Reserve in Victoria. The walking trail at this park had been my sanctuary during the summer of 2011 as I awaited my upcoming sentencing hearing date to arrive in November. It was a place where God spoke to my heart. It was where he told me

I was in the way of everything he needed to accomplish in the heart of Milt, the man with whom I'd had an adulterous affair. And a few months after that, God gave me the strength to end our relationship. Five years had passed since I'd walked this park, and Milt had recently completed his prison sentence.

I retraced my steps around the four-mile trail and celebrated how far I had come. I also wondered if God had indeed accomplished a mighty work in Milt's heart during his incarceration. When I reached the top of the hill, where I met my angel years ago (a story captured in *Call Me Vivian*), I simply gave God the glory and thanked him for everything he had done in my life. I felt at peace as I reunited with a little piece of my past.

I spent a relaxing weekend with my son and grandsons, and on Monday morning I drove to Seedlings, a small Christian bookstore in Chanhassen. A few years prior, an acquaintance suggested that I check it out, and I'm so glad that I did. I introduced myself to the owner, Janice, who turned out to be involved in a number of ministries and knew a group of ladies who did prison ministry at the women's Minnesota Correctional Facility in nearby Shakopee.

On this visit, I brought with me marketing materials for my book, including "Heaven Cent" poems, which contained information about *Call Me Vivian* and The Vivian Foundation. I hoped to convince Janice to put them into the bags of customers.

When I entered the store, I did not see Janice, so I browsed the tables and shelves for a few minutes and struck up a casual conversation with a younger, well-dressed woman who was shopping. Janice heard my voice and emerged from her office. "What are you doing here?" she asked, looking surprised but happy to see me.

"I'm visiting my family, but the Holy Spirit sent me here with some marketing materials."

"But why today? Why now?" she pressed as she walked toward the woman and me. Janice must have registered the confusion on my face because she continued before I had a chance to reply.

"Katie, I would like you to meet someone. This is the woman from my church who I told you about."

Janice had told me long ago about this woman and her husband. Janice said the Lord put them on her heart every time she saw them, and she sensed something amiss given the amount of weight the wife had lost. Initially, Janice thought she might have had an illness of some sort, but she eventually learned that a judge had sentenced the woman's husband to an extended stay at a federal prison in Duluth, Minnesota. After Janice told me this, she helped arrange a phone call, and I ended up speaking to the husband the evening prior to his surrender.

Are you kidding me, Lord? I thought now. His hand in orchestrating this introduction was plain to see, and as usual, none of us saw it coming. It didn't take long for Janice to suggest that the woman and I move elsewhere to talk more privately.

This woman, who found solace in the bookstore, tearfully explained how she felt like her world was crumbling around her. Her eyes shone with tears, and she looked defeated. She wondered how she was supposed to get through the day, let alone care for their four kids by herself. It had only been a short time since her husband left to begin serving his five-year prison sentence, and she and her kids were preparing for one of their first visits to the correctional facility. I shared with her what they could expect upon arrival in addition to the rules and regulations of a prison visiting room.

I encouraged her as best I could and asked her to consider her situation from a kingdom perspective. Then I shared all of the good that had come out of my incarceration and assured her that her family would be fine despite their challenging circumstances. "God sent so many people to help me," I told her. "I can look back on those two years in prison and tell you that every bit of it was necessary to transform my heart and ultimately prepare me for my divine destiny."

I am not sure if she believed me, but maybe all this woman needed that day was a long embrace and an opportunity to pour out her pain and heartache to someone who could relate to her struggles. We prayed together, asking God to protect their family. As I left the store and headed toward my car, I shook my head in disbelief. Once again, God directed my steps, and I thanked him for the opportunity to serve as the hands and feet of Jesus. I never learned whether the marketing materials ended up in the bags of customers, but I hoped and prayed that my thirty-minute conversation with my new friend encouraged her to look for the good that God would make of her unimaginably difficult circumstances.

God orchestrated a number of other divine appointments with people from whom I could learn and grow while I was in Minnesota. I met with Tahni Cullen and John Turnipseed, fellow BroadStreet Publishing authors. Tahni's book, *Josiah's Fire*, chronicles her family's journey with their son, Josiah, who has autism. Josiah was nonverbal and had never formally learned to read or write, but one day, he suddenly began typing profound messages about God and heaven on his iPad.

John Turnipseed is the author of *Bloodline*, a gripping story about his life as a former gang leader, pimp, and drug dealer. Today, John works with Five Stone Media, a Christian nonprofit, and he's also the director of the nationally recognized Fathering Center at Urban Ventures, another faith-based nonprofit located in the heart of Minneapolis and within the very same neighborhood that John used to terrorize.

After ten productive days in Minnesota, it was time for me to head home. Soon after my return, I felt in my spirit that I would hear from Milt. Just one day later, a friend called to tell me that Milt had showed up at her place of employment in Florida. We talked about their meeting and left it at that. Still, I wondered again whether Milt had changed as much as I had. Then in October, I attended an especially uplifting church service in which we focused on Ephesians 4:15–16:

We will speak the truth in love, growing in every way more and more like Christ, who is the head of his body, the church. He makes the whole body fit together perfectly. As each part does its own special work, it helps the other parts grow, so that the whole body is healthy and growing and full of love.

I love the message found in these verses: We are all gifted with talents and abilities to serve the Lord. One such God-given ability is the gift of prophecy. And as the worship portion of the service ended, a young woman in her early thirties with shoulder-length hair approached the microphone to say that she had been given a word of knowledge from the Lord. For whatever reason, I felt compelled to use my phone to record what she said.

I woke up this morning remembering the verse that talks about not being burdened again by a yoke of slavery. I was also thinking about a time in my life when I walked away from the Lord, and the common term for that is backsliding. So if that resonates with you, please listen closely.

I believe there are one or two people here who God specifically wants to speak to today. I felt him saying, "Don't be burdened again by the things that burdened you in the past." And I believe that there's a person here specifically who has a relationship that they are tempted to go back to, and probably not in the same way that it was in the past. But it's possibly something like a long-distance thing, like "I want to go visit this person."

If there's somebody here who's planning a trip to visit an old friend or somebody who they were romantically involved with in the past, and you've been wondering if it's right, thinking, *I think this is okay. I think this is right. It's a good friendship*, then I believe the word of the Lord to you is, "Don't do it. Don't go."

His answer to you is no, and if you've heard nothing else today about him wanting to equip you to walk in righteousness and to say no to ungodliness, hear this now. He says no. It's a directive full of love. It's a directive full of grace. He's not mad at you; he just wants you to know it clearly.

I believe for somebody else it's something to do with past addiction—drugs, alcohol, anything that we can be addicted to. If you woke up this morning or sometime in the past week and contemplated going somewhere, doing something, whatever it might be, and you've found yourself thinking, *I think I can handle this. I think it's going to be okay. I think I'm beyond where I was,* then I believe the word of the Lord to you is, "Don't do it." And once again, I believe he says that out of love, compassion, and grace. He wants to protect you and keep you in a safe place, but his answer is no.

What this young woman did not realize was that this was one message, not two, and it was intended for me based on the prayers I had lifted up to the Lord. This message reminded me that God wants to promote us, but we must stay focused on him and his perfect plan for our lives. We must walk in obedience. We cannot reach the next level without maturity, and maturity in Christ comes from loving and serving our Lord. It comes from doing the hard things and resisting temptations. And most importantly, it's about answering God's call and allowing his perfect plan to play out in our lives.

Typically, whenever God wants me to do something, he is persistent. I had received three invitations to Bible studies, and he was making it quite obvious that he wanted me to attend a particular study at Grace Church in Racine. Wanting to be obedient, I showed up and walked in with an attitude of expectancy.

It was a Thursday morning and the first day of December. I spoke to the team leader upon my arrival and told him about *Call Me Vivian,* The Vivian Foundation, and the "Just One Word Bible Reading Plans." He thanked me for coming, and I was surprised that nearly fifty people were in attendance. As the study ended, the team leader introduced me to the group. He also encouraged the attendees to stop by the table at which I was seated if they were interested in the foundation's resources. I thought nearly everyone would be interested since God was adamant about me attending this event, yet as the room emptied, I wondered if perhaps that wasn't God's plan at all.

Then Roy and Sophia, who usually attended a different church called Hope Community Church, stopped by to chat. I gave each of them a copy of my book, and Roy was excited to get his hands on the "Just One Word Bible Reading Plans."

"I help with the kids at our church," Roy explained, "and I had no idea what I was going to do tonight. These resources are perfect."

"Come and see us sometime," Sophia chimed in as they walked toward the door.

Two weeks later, on my way home from the gym, I stopped by Hope Community Church to drop off the newest Bible reading plan. I was still sweaty, but I planned to be quick about it. I met the church secretary, Ann, who thanked me for coming by. But as I was heading out of the door, in walked the pastor, and I didn't know whether I should laugh or run for cover. He introduced himself as Pastor Sam.

"They say there's never a second chance to make a first impression," I said as I sheepishly shook his hand. Then I explained how I had just finished an intense workout and promised that I would look and smell better the next time he saw me. We had a great forty-five minute discussion, and I felt completely at ease with Pastor Sam and the church secretary despite my less-than-stunning appearance. I sensed that God was in motion.

The following Sunday, I visited Hope Community Church a second time, and the worship experience was far different from Living Light Church. For one thing, the congregation was much smaller, and that simple observation got me thinking about the concept of training. When we undergo any type of training, there are always parts that we don't necessarily like, especially when we're working to physically improve our bodies. In some ways, spiritual training is similar. It can be uncomfortable, but it's necessary if we want to learn and grow. When we get too comfortable with a certain routine or a certain group of people, we may not challenge ourselves to the extent that we should.

I listened to Pastor Sam that Sunday as he spoke on the faith of Mary and Joseph and their obedience to God. Then the gentleman sitting next to me told me that the Lord had a specific Scripture for me that day, which also appeared on the front of the program: "'For I know the plans I have for you,' says the LORD. 'They are plans for good and not for disaster, to give you a future and a hope'" (Jeremiah 29:11). The same man then handed me a small, black and red boxing glove about six inches tall with the message "Fight for your dreams" printed in white lettering.

That same evening, I had a dream. In it, I was asked to do something that I knew I could do, but it had been a long time since I had done this particular task. In my dream, I said, "I know I can do it, but I need some training." To most people that might not seem like a big deal, but that parting comment carried great significance. I understood that God was telling me that I needed additional training, and it would take place at Hope Community Church. It was time to step out in faith. I had been sensing in my spirit for some time that God was preparing to move me to a new church, so it was an easy decision to accept his invitation.

In all honesty, I dream vividly every night, and God often uses numbers to direct me to Scripture. At the time, the consistent theme of my dreams had been wisdom. James 1:5 tells us, "If you need wisdom, then ask our generous God, and he will give it to you. He will not rebuke you for asking." The word *wisdom* in this verse does not simply refer to knowledge; it also implies that we should ask God to help us make wise decisions in difficult circumstances.

The study notes in the NLT Parallel Study Bible tell us that wisdom has three distinct characteristics.

1. It is practical. The wisdom from God relates to life even during the most trying times. It is not wisdom isolated from suffering and trials. This wisdom is the tool by which trials are overcome. An intelligent person may have profound ideas, but a wise person puts profound ideas into practice.

2. It is divine. God's wisdom goes beyond common sense. Common sense does not lead us to choose joy in the middle of trials. This wisdom begins with respect for God, leads to living by God's direction, and results in the ability to tell right from wrong.

3. It is Christlike. Asking for wisdom is ultimately asking to be like Christ. The Bible identifies Christ as the "wisdom of God" (1 Corinthians 1:24; 2:1–7).[8]

Proverbs 2:2–6 provides additional insight on wisdom.

Tune your ears to wisdom, and concentrate on understanding. Cry out for insight, and ask for understanding. Search for them as you would for silver; seek them like hidden treasures. Then you will understand what it means to fear the LORD, and you will gain knowledge of God. For the LORD grants wisdom! From his mouth come knowledge and understanding.

We gain this understanding by spending time in God's Word, praying, and making the most of the teachable moments that he strategically places in our lives. God's promises are found in his Word, which is why we have to spend time in the Bible. Once we know his Word, we can use those promises in prayer. Prayer becomes powerful when you speak God's promises into existence, and it's a great way to beat Satan at his own game.

We also gain wisdom by looking at things though God's eyes. We may not always like where he's placed us or even what he has asked us to do, but we must remember that he only wants the best for his children. And sometimes, the lessons we learn when we're stretched beyond our comfort zone are the best lessons of all because they impart godly wisdom.

Even though I didn't know anyone at Hope Community Church except for one former coworker, I was looking forward to attending their Christmas party in a couple of weeks. When the time came, I wondered if they would cancel the event due to a significant snowstorm. Nevertheless, I put on a pair of my nicer jeans and a red sweater and headed to church, feeling both happy and relieved to find cars in the parking lot. Although I felt a little nervous walking in, I had a great time and shared delicious food with wonderful people. I was amazed at how quickly I felt at home and knew that I was right where the Lord wanted me.

That night, I thought back on the day's events. I was pretty certain that I would eventually be given an opportunity to speak at my new church, and I was right. That door would open on numerous occasions. I would be a guest speaker at their women's luncheon and was asked to lead Bible study. And on many Sundays, the Lord had me share words of knowledge with the congregation.

Hope Community Church went on to partner with The Vivian Foundation, and thousands of Christian books were sown into other ministries as a result of where the Lord placed me. Once again, God made it obvious that I was exactly where he needed me. Now it was up to me to make the most of this opportunity.

5

I visit the post office almost every day. My PO box rests on the top row in the far left-hand corner, so I have to stand on my tip-toes to unlock it. Every time I turn the key, I'm hoping and praying that I'll find financial provisions for The Vivian Foundation. And if the box is empty, I have a tradition in which I thank God for the checks that are on the way.

One day, I opened the box to find a notice that postage was due for something sent from Redgranite Correctional Institute in central Wisconsin. The clerk retrieved the box, and I paid what was owed before returning to my car. I opened the parcel and out popped out a big sign written in red and green marker that read, "Surprise! Merry Christmas to The Vivian Foundation and God Bless Racine Wisconsin." Hand-drawn Christmas trees and smiley faces adorned the heartfelt card.

The package turned out to be from Antoine, an inmate God had placed in my path six months earlier. Antoine was from Racine, Wisconsin, and had been incarcerated since the age of nineteen. He had read *Call Me Vivian*, and we remained in touch ever since, serving as encouragement to one another. By the time I met him, he'd spent more than twenty years in prison.

Also inside the box from Antoine were eleven knit hats for children, two crocheted teddy bears, and handcrafted ornaments. Because of his kindness, the foundation was able to bless kids with Christmas gifts. His note continued, "Merry Christmas, Katie. May

God bless the giving away of the enclosed gifts. I pray they fit. God, stretch the hats if need be. In Jesus' name. Amen. Continue to find pleasure in God." On the back of the card were two verses.

> Pure and genuine religion in the sight of God the Father means caring for orphans and widows in their distress and refusing to let the world corrupt you. (James 1:27)

> "I will protect the orphans who remain among you. Your widows, too, can depend on me for help." (Jeremiah 49:11)

A few months later, Antoine sent me a card filled with godly wisdom. Truer words have never been spoken. He wrote about spiritual storms and how they have a way of depositing wisdom in our spirit, love in our heart, trust in our soul, eternal perspective in our eyes, praise in our mouth, joy in our being, and more of Jesus in our life. Antoine also included a quote from Dr. Charles Stanley of In Touch Ministries: "When the storms of life batter you, make sure your feet are planted on the solid rock of Jesus Christ. Do not despair, asking, what am I going to do? Rather, ask, what is God doing? And be assured, he is doing something."

My phone rang two weeks later, and when I looked down at the caller ID, I saw that it was none other than Dale, the prophetess from Coleman. Dale reaches out to me quite often at the prompting of the Holy Spirit, and whenever we talk, God reveals specific messages for me. As I shared with her what I had been up to, including some marketing ideas for The Vivian Foundation, she interrupted me. "Katie," Dale said, "God needs you to slow down. He wants you to go to that secret place and listen." She went on to describe my pace with the foundation like "the tortoise and the hare."

I couldn't help but burst out laughing because every time someone asked me how things were going, I'd respond, "Slow and steady." If you don't remember Aesop's fable about the tortoise and the hare, here's a quick recap.

The Hare was one boasting of his speed before the other animals. "I have never yet been beaten," said he, "when I put forth my full speed. I challenge any one here to race with me."

The Tortoise said quietly, "I accept your challenge."

"That is a good joke," said the Hare; "I could dance around you all the way."

"Keep your boasting till you've won," answered the Tortoise. "Shall we race?"

So a course was fixed and a start was made. The Hare darted almost out of sight at once, but soon stopped and, to show contempt for the Tortoise, lay down to have a nap. The Tortoise plodded on and on, and when the Hare awoke from his nap, he saw the Tortoise just near the winning-post and could not run up in time to save the race.

Then the Tortoise said, "Slow and steady progress wins the race."[9]

God was impressing upon me that I must slow down, focus, and remain in step with the Holy Spirit. I've casually observed several ministries that wanted to move faster than God appeared to intend because he always brought them back to where they started. Their hearts were in the right place; their plans, enthusiasm, and passion for growing their cause were admirable and yet never materialized. In ministry and in life, when we try to do things in our own strength, we often fail. And while failure can be a great teaching tool, we must do things God's way if we want to be successful. We must be patient and willing to wait on him to make things happen.

Then, the last week of December, I received a message from a former inmate that confirmed Dale's heavenly directive: "Dear Woman of God, be still for a while and praise God for his favor, his grace, and his awesomeness. God is able to do the impossible and is always near. Praise him with one voice. Amen."

I consciously worked on slowing down as God instructed. A friend of mine reached out and shared that her family was experiencing challenges, so I met up with her at a local coffee shop to offer reassurance. As we were talking, she asked if I had any plans for the winter.

"Well, I'd like to spend a few months in Florida," I told her, "but I'm not sure if that is a part of God's plan." Whenever I'm at a crossroads, I ask God to reveal exactly what he wants me to do. My prayer is simple and straight forward: *God make it so obvious that I can't miss it!*

Not thinking much about my conversation with my friend earlier that day, I received a phone call from Linda, a friend in Florida from whom I rented a room whenever I visited. Linda called to tell me that she had taken in a long-term tenant, which meant my bedroom would no longer be available.

My friend Paula introduced me to Linda years earlier at a New Year's Eve party that Linda attended with her husband, Ron. At the time, I was days away from beginning my prison sentence at Coleman, and the four of us found ourselves at a gathering that I can only describe as bizarre. To this day, we laugh about that night and how we couldn't get out of there fast enough. None of us made it to midnight! Five years after this fateful meeting, God brought Linda and me back together after Ron passed away. Linda was coping well but needed a roommate, and living together was a beneficial arrangement for both of us.

Sharing living space with Linda came easily and effortlessly, and our friendship blossomed. We shared much-needed laughter and tears of grief as we both came to terms with everything life had thrown at us. In hindsight, it's clear that God's hand orchestrated all of it. My first book contract came through within the first year of us living together, and I even held the foundation's first board of directors meeting while seated at Linda's dining room table.

For most of her life, Linda was the primary caregiver for her mother, who moved into Linda's home when she and Ron first married. Then in the last twenty years of their marriage, Ron developed significant health issues, too, which doubled Linda's caregiving duties. Instead of complaining or buckling under the pressure, Linda took things one day at a time and cared for her mother and husband with dignity, grace, and confidence that their care was part of God's plan for her life.

I had been just weeks away from driving to the Sunshine State, but the Lord had confirmed to me through Linda's tenant news that Florida was not in his plan for me. Of course, I was disappointed, but I knew he had a reason. Meanwhile, letters continued to fill my mailbox from inmates who read *Call Me Vivian*. I was averaging ten to fifteen letters per week from prisons around the country, including ongoing correspondence with an inmate named Amy. Amy was in a county jail in Dresden, Tennessee, and in the midst of her fifth stay in jail. She shared her life story with me, revealing her struggle with addiction, the pain from her divorce, and the tragic loss of her son. She would yo-yo between highs and lows and periods of sobriety and addiction, but she never lost sight of the Lord.

> All this time I have been convinced that addiction was my problem. God has finally shown me through your book that addiction is only a symptom of a much bigger issue: codependency...I have never been more thankful to be surrounded by [God's] presence in the confines of a cell. Each morning I place my plastic shoes beneath my knees and war for my life, and like you, God speaks to me through his Word and through books.

I talked to Amy upon her release and encouraged her to let God continue to direct her steps. The Vivian Foundation also forwarded two cases of Christian books to Amy as she began her ministry efforts at her local church.

Just before 2016 came to an end, I asked God for a financial blessing to come to The Vivian Foundation in an usual way. I honestly wasn't sure what I meant by that, but then we received a donation from a woman named Audrey who lived in the Baltimore area. Her donation was the first contribution we'd received from someone I personally did not know.

Audrey told me in a letter that she had read my book and that my story moved her. She lived on a fixed income but would save money so that she could bless a few special ministries at the end of every year. Given Audrey's love for children, God touched her heart with the mission of The Vivian Foundation, and she sent a money order our way. She also purchased six additional copies of *Call Me Vivian* to give away as Christmas gifts. Audrey also told me about a Christmas card ministry that she had started a few years earlier, and I immediately thought of our "Heaven Cent" poems. I crafted a letter, grabbed six of my books, and dropped one hundred poems in the mail to Audrey.

About a week later, I received from Audrey a second letter thanking me, and she also detailed the origin story of her Christmas card ministry. After closing her in-home day care and retiring in her early seventies, Audrey struggled financially. She turned to the Lord, asking him what she should do next, and she felt led to give out Christmas cards to celebrate Jesus' birthday.

> In three years or more, I've only encountered three people who refused a Christmas card. Most people are really pleased. Me, I'm overjoyed doing this work for the Lord. I make a funny figure. An old lady in her eighties chasing people through Wal-Mart asking if they want a Christmas card…Without the joy of the Lord, I would be a weak-kneed, sorry old lady. But praise God, Jesus holds my hand wherever I go.

Audrey mailed a few more letters to me, and they always put a smile on my face. She told me she wants to be a warrior for Christ but is sometimes a "wimp," so God led her to Ephesians 3:14–21, which she began to use as her daily prayer. She further reminded me that "Paul told Timothy to stir himself up," which was why she regularly wrote out Scripture; it allowed God to talk to her through his Word. "I personalize the verses and I try to learn them," she explained. "The truth of Scripture is not changed. But I take that truth to build a stronger, god-like person within myself."

I learned so much from Audrey, and she always kept me on my toes. She once told me she was building a prayer room in her basement and that she planned to paint it hot pink. The last letter I received from her read, "Dear friend, when we can truly get God's wonderful words into our hearts, minds, and innermost parts of our souls, we will be unshakeable by our circumstances. For we'll truly know the C in Christ is bigger than the c in our circumstances." Eighty-three-year-old Audrey left a legacy of love. I told her I was convinced that she would appear in my next book, and I was right.

Many prison ministries, including The Vivian Foundation, do not have the money needed to accomplish everything they set out to do. With limited funds in the foundation's bank account, I decided to plan a fundraiser. I worked out a plan with my publisher and purchased over a thousand copies of various books and devotionals that they published. My plan was to use these books to solicit donations and raise money to print a coloring booklet by The Vivian Foundation.

At the same time, I heard from two ministries that were requesting quantities of the same type of resources I had just purchased. Although I bought these books to raise money for The Vivian Foundation, God was making it quite clear that I was to meet the needs of these organizations. And I know what God does with his Word: "I send it out, and it always produces fruit. It will accomplish all I want it to, and it will prosper everywhere I send it" (Isaiah 55:11). If God was going to use these books to bear fruit, I was not going to argue with him. I had to be obedient, so I shipped the books to North Carolina and Florida and put our fundraising efforts on hold.

Less than a week after donating the books I'd purchased for fundraising purposes, I received an email from Carlton Garborg, the president of BroadStreet Publishing, which published *Call Me Vivian*. Carlton wrote that the company had a "Scooby Snack" for me and was donating thousands of books to The Vivian Foundation. I thought of 2 Corinthians and its lesson on giving.

> You must each decide in your heart how much to give. And don't give reluctantly or in response to pressure. "For God loves a person who gives cheerfully." And God will generously provide all you need. Then you will always have everything you need and plenty left over to share with others. As the Scriptures say, "They share freely and give generously to the poor. Their good deeds will be remembered forever." For God is the one who provides seed for the farmer and then bread to eat. In the same way he will provide and increase your resources and then produce a great harvest of generosity in you. Yes, you will be enriched in every way so that you can always be generous. And when we take your gifts to those who need them, they will thank God. (9:7–11)

When I had no money to purchase additional resources, God once again opened the windows of heaven and poured out a blessing so great that The Vivian Foundation had plenty to share with others. We blessed numerous ministries throughout the country with hundreds of thousands of dollars of retail inventory and raised enough money to print The Vivian Foundation coloring booklet.

God knew all along that he was going to give me a book ministry and lined everything up well in advance. What was the chance that my publisher, with its corporate offices located in Savage, Minnesota, would warehouse their books in Racine, Wisconsin, just fifteen minutes away from my home?

In early March of 2017, a news station out of Chicago ran a powerful story about mothers in prison and children of incarcerated parents, highlighting the heartache and pain that these kids suffer. The segment poignantly questioned who is truly punished in the end. It was an easy decision for me to share this video on social media. Then Regina, a friend from prison, saw this post and asked me if this was a problem in our state of Wisconsin. I hated to have to respond the way that I did, but I knew it was important.

> It's a problem in every state. Ten percent of the 2.3 million inmates in the U.S. are women. Plus, 2.7 million children have a mother or father in prison, and half of those kids are under the age of ten. One in every 28 kids has experienced parental incarceration. Unfortunately, given the cost and distance associated with prison visits, [nearly] 60 percent of inmates [who are mothers and fathers] never receive a visit [from their children].[10] It's a very big problem, which is why The Vivian Foundation supports ministries that are in the trenches helping these families.

Regina's reply not only included a wonderfully generous compliment, but it also shared godly wisdom: "What grieves you is a clue to something that you are assigned to heal. Compassion is a signpost." God is a God of mercy and compassion, and Jesus always showed compassion toward others. Compassion shares in the suffering of others. It is a type of sympathy that is usually reserved for unusual or distressing circumstances.

Our marching orders are clear: We must have the attitude of Christ. I pondered Regina's message and realized the importance of paying attention to the things that break our hearts. This can direct our steps toward showing mercy and compassion to others: "Make me truly happy by agreeing wholeheartedly with each other, loving one another, and working together with one mind and purpose" (Philippians 2:2).

Regina's message also reminded me of our time together in prison, and I thought back to one particular evening when we discussed the characteristics of true biblical leaders. There are seven biblical models of leadership from which we can learn.

1. Paul: "Believe in something bigger than yourself."
2. Nehemiah: "Build on what God has given you."
3. Joshua: "Bring the best people to the table."
4. Barnabas: "Bridge the gaps of differing opinions."
5. Moses: "Blind your eyes to petty criticism."
6. Elijah: "Bind the ties of love and courage."
7. Peter: "Bounce back after you are knocked down."[11]

These were all great men of faith whom God used to positively impact our lives. But there's much to learn from women in the Bible too. Let's focus on Deborah, one of the most famous women in the Old Testament. Deborah was an extraordinary woman: a wife, a prophetess, an outstanding leader, and a judge who was not only known for her wisdom but was also recognized for her courage.

As a prophetess, Deborah discerned and declared the mind of God. She ministered as a mediator between God and his people. She poured out his wisdom, knowledge, and instruction when people came to her for help, and God used her to ignite a spiritual revival in the hearts of his people and to bring the Israelites back to him. Deborah's remarkable wisdom showed itself through her humility. She did not seek to become a judge or to lead people. She found greatness in God's kingdom by following the path of humble service—never seeking and never being too aggressive or too assertive. Deborah waited on God, encouraged others to lead, and assisted when needed.

As individuals, we can and should mirror Deborah's leadership. Like her, we must answer God's call and commit to serving others, understanding the people he wants us to support, developing the capacity to share his love with compassion, and doing all of this with confidence in the God whom we serve. Like her, we must display courage when we step out in faith, have conviction in our belief of God's Word, and trust in his promises.

We all have special gifts, talents, and abilities to serve the Lord. I have learned that God will call us into places that we never could have imagined, and he will equip us to accomplish things we never thought ourselves capable of doing. Our job is to walk in obedience and serve others in love. Trust God's perfect plan. He will lead the way; he always does.

6

The automotive insurance premium arrived for the new Buick Encore. The premium was quite a bit higher than what I typically paid, and the increase in rates left me frustrated. This was the vehicle God had put me in, so this must have been the car he intended me to drive. Or was it? I had learned a long time ago to never look a gift horse in the mouth, but my spirit was restless over this vehicle.

When I shared my displeasure over the insurance cost with my girlfriends, they told me to "stop complaining" about my free car. Two days after that discussion, I shared my restlessness with another friend and reiterated the agitation in my spirit: "I don't know if this is God or the devil, but my restlessness over this vehicle will not go away." I even reached out to the gentleman who so generously gave me the car, asking him if the time was right to make a move. "I want to be prudent," I told him. "Please don't think that I do not appreciate your gift. I just want to make sure that I'm being a good steward of what I have been given."

As I continued contemplating, another vehicle on the dealership's website caught my eye. It was a new Ford Edge, and with rebates, it was nearly $8,000 below the manufacturer's suggested retail price. I wondered if God was guiding me toward a larger vehicle due to the foundation's growing needs. We needed cargo space for our fundraising activities and ministry efforts.

I couldn't get the vehicle off my mind, and luckily, the dealership with the Ford Edge was on the way to an upcoming lunch date I had with a friend in Illinois. I figured it wouldn't hurt to take a quick look at the car, so I left a little earlier than I had planned. Practicing what I preached, I prayed over the next few days that if God wanted me to change vehicles, then he needed to make it painfully obvious. I wanted to stay within his perfect will, so my prayer, which is one that I have prayed many times, was, *God, hit me over the head with a two-by-four so that I know exactly what to do.*

I arrived at the dealership at nine o'clock on Monday morning. The dealership was fairly quiet at that hour, and a salesperson named Anthony greeted me. I explained to him that I was interested in the discounted Ford Edge. He found the SUV, but since I hadn't given them advance notice of my interest, let's just say the vehicle was not as clean as it could have been. It even had a small ding near the gas tank. God knew that ding alone would steer me away from that vehicle, and he was right.

As Anthony and I strolled the lot, I felt compelled to tell him about my book and a little bit more about my background, including my time in prison. He hung his head and told me that we shared similar backgrounds. Anthony had spent three years in prison, and just six weeks before he surrendered, his son was born. I knew then that this was a divine appointment. I grabbed a few books from the Buick, and when I went back inside, I learned that another one of the dealership's sales guys, John, had also spent time in jail. John could not believe it when Anthony told him that I founded a nonprofit for children of incarcerated parents.

A few minutes later and much to my surprise, another employee showed up, and I recognized him from my hometown. This gentleman, Jason, had sold a car to our family five years ago and was now the sales manager of this dealership; I had no idea he even worked there! I was hit by a two-by-four—just as I'd prayed. It was obvious that God was up to something.

We started to chat, and I explained to Jason that, among other issues, the cargo capacity of the Buick was not always adequate. We discussed the bump in insurance rates, the value of the Buick, and the need for a larger vehicle that would better meet the foundation's needs. I wondered out loud if the time was right to leverage the equity in the Encore and innocently asked, "Do you have any creative solutions?"

To make a long story short, I took the equity in the Buick, applied it to a two-year, one-pay lease on a new Ford Escape, and the foundation received a nice check for the Buick's remaining value. The check's amount and the debt on our balance sheet were identical. A quick call to my insurance agent confirmed a lower insurance premium on the new vehicle. In one fell swoop, God secured a larger vehicle and paid the foundation's startup expenses.

While the car was being detailed, Anthony and I talked more. He told me he was disappointed about "a lucrative job opportunity" that he had recently missed out on.

"Anthony," I started, "God's Word in Revelation 3:7 tells us that God can open a door that no man can shut and shut a door that no man can open. If God wanted you to get that job, then that door would have opened. You need to trust him. He has something so much better for you."

Tears welled in Anthony's eyes. I felt the Holy Spirit hovering and guiding my words as I continued, "Sometimes God protects us, and sometimes our hearts just aren't ready. God will not let us move forward until he has our heart where he wants it."

I felt as though I'd won the lottery. Not only did God direct my steps to bless me in an unexpected manner, but I also had an opportunity to bless Anthony with God's wisdom. Once the SUV was ready and the license plates changed, I hopped in and drove to my lunch date.

After lunch, I decided to return home before dark. I headed east on a four-lane highway in Kenosha County and quickly noticed a sheriff's squad car behind me. The speed limit on this particular stretch of road was set to fifty-five miles per hour, so I hovered between fifty and fifty-five in the left lane. The squad car stayed glued to my rear bumper for about ten minutes before its lights began to flash. I pulled to the side of the road, not knowing what to expect.

I reached for the paperwork for the new car, looked over my left shoulder, and saw the police officer approaching my window. His badge revealed his name was Sergeant Gonzales of the Kenosha Police Department.

"Good evening, Miss," Sergeant Gonzales started. "Did you realize you were driving too slowly for the left lane?"

I laughed and said, "Well, you were right behind me, and I didn't want to get a ticket."

"I was hoping you would pull into the right lane since you were driving slower than everyone else. The cars were backing up behind me."

I laughed a little harder, realizing I had officially become my grandpa, who was notorious for driving ten to fifteen miles below the speed limit.

Sergeant Gonzales examined my registration and asked about The Vivian Foundation, seeing as the vehicle is registered in the foundation's name. I told him about our mission of helping children of incarcerated parents and mentioned our outreach program for inmates. I also mentioned *Call Me Vivian*.

Sergeant Gonzales shared that he, too, was a believer, and I knew with certainty that this encounter was more than a traffic stop; it was another two-by-four moment.

"One of the other reasons I pulled you over is because your plates are registered to a Buick Encore."

"Yes, officer," I replied. "I traded in the Buick for this Ford Escape just this morning." That became all the more obvious when I tried to turn off my blinker and mistakenly turned on the windshield wipers.

We talked more about the foundation and its resources, and we agreed on two things: I would no longer drive in the left lane, and I would drop off hundreds of ministry resources at the Kenosha Police Department for their chaplain.

God truly works in mysterious ways. As Proverbs 16:9 reads, "We can make our plans, but the LORD determines our steps." For over a week, my spirit had stirred over a new car. Then I drive to a dealership in a city that I have never visited only to find not one but two salesmen who were former inmates and a sales manager whom I personally knew. I walk out with a new car without payments, no maintenance costs for two years, a reduced insurance premium, and a check large enough to cover the foundation's debt. I get a prompting in my spirit to head home before dark, and an hour into my ride, a police officer—who happens to be a Christian—pulls right behind me and decides to run a check on my license plate. Had Sergeant Gonzales not stopped me, the inmates at the facilities in Kenosha would not have resources from the Vivian Foundation to learn more about a saving relationship with Jesus Christ.

Since the new car was a Ford Escape, I felt compelled to look up the word *escape* in the Bible. The traditional definition of *escape* is to "break free from confinement or control."[12] The biblical definition of this word is "to avoid, to get free of, or break away."[13] Luke 21:36 reminds us to stay alert at all times and pray that we are strong enough to escape the coming horrors when we stand before the Son of Man. To "stand before" means to pass the test. In other words, we need to work faithfully at the tasks God has given us because we will not escape his judgment. Or as Peter wrote,

> Make every effort to respond to God's promises. Supplement your faith with a generous provision of moral excellence, and moral excellence with knowledge, and knowledge with self-control, and self-control with patient endurance, and patient endurance with godliness, and godliness with brotherly affection, and brotherly affection with love for everyone.

The more you grow like this, the more productive and useful you will be in your knowledge of our Lord Jesus Christ. But those who fail to develop in this way are shortsighted or blind, forgetting they have been cleansed from their old sins. So, dear brothers and sisters, work hard to prove that you really are among those God has called and chosen. Do these things and you will never fall away. Then God will give you a grand entrance into the eternal Kingdom of our Lord and Savior Jesus Christ. (2 Peter 1:5–11)

Sometimes we do not always see the direction God intends for us to go. Back in 2015, as I mentioned earlier, a woman had prophetically spoken to me, "Books, books, books. I see many books. Some of these are already in the library of heaven. The Holy Spirit will write these, but you are the vessel." At the time, I thought that message referred only to my books, but I received a text message in 2017 from a friend who wanted to know if I was interested in writing a book for a former inmate. Since then, at least a dozen other inmates have asked me to help them write their stories. Their kind words humble me, but I decided to stay in my own lane relative to my ministry calling. I declined for a couple of reasons the opportunity from the friend who texted me. First, the timing was not right; The Vivian Foundation had me so busy. Second, it didn't feel right for me to co-author another person's story.

A few weeks after telling my friend that I did not have the time to help this woman write her book, God told me otherwise. Remaining obedient to my latest heavenly directive, I asked my friend for her contact information. Her name was Hannah, and almost two months passed before the two of us finally met at a coffee shop. After sharing a little bit about my experiences and giving her a copy of *Call Me Vivian*, Hannah started to open up and share her childhood with me. The more she talked, the more I listened, and my pen could hardly keep up with the pace of her memory as she revealed the shocking events of her life.

Hannah endured a childhood that no youngster should ever experience. She suffered horrific abuse at the hands of the very people who were supposed to love and nurture her, and she was all too familiar with the revolving door of prison. Her grief and anger regarding her upbringing were pent up yet so tangible. And while she was able to talk openly about what transpired, she said she had no idea how to get her thoughts on paper.

It became clear that my role was to support and encourage Hannah in any way that I could by listening and learning more about her life. Additionally, I was to provide her a solid framework from which she could creatively begin her story and to offer suggestions on how to incorporate teachable moments into her life experiences. I took copious notes so that I could take elements and details from our initial meeting and craft them into an introduction.

As soon as I returned home, I began writing while the information was fresh in my mind. After less than two hours, I finished the prologue to Hannah's story. I couldn't believe it. My writing was effortless, which is exactly what happens when the Holy Spirit takes over. After reading what I had written, I knew with certainty that this was the start of something special.

Of course, God's intervention in my life did not stop there. In late March of 2017, I connected with the new chaplain at the Racine County Jail. Imagine my surprise when I learned he was a spirit-filled, apostolic pastor whom God had called into this position to take back the territory from the devil. This God-fearing man was walking in step with the Spirit, which became obvious as we spoke more.

"God is sending people into some very dark places," the chaplain said. "Whatever we accomplish will create a template that will be repeated with success in other prisons."

It also became apparent that the Holy Spirit was speaking through both of us, especially about God's favor. The chaplain received a prophetic word for me while I shared my testimony with him: "God has not showed you your complete destiny—only a glimpse of the destination. Your destiny is hidden in a secret place because once he reveals it, the devil will attack."

God was all over this divine appointment and continuing to open new doors. I dropped off copies of my book and ministry resources at the Racine County Jail, and *Call Me Vivian* would eventually find its way into the hands of maximum security inmates. I was also able to provide my books and other Christian resources to the Racine Correctional Facility, which houses male inmates, as well as the Robert E. Ellsworth Correctional Center for Women.

An even more exciting opportunity presented itself for me to speak at the Milwaukee Women's Correctional Center, and it all started on an airplane. The flight from Milwaukee to Tampa was full, and as I searched for a seat (this was a Southwest flight), the flight attendant spoke over the speaker, "Please sit down immediately in the closest available seat. This flight is full."

I looked to my right and saw a woman who kind of reminded me of myself: similar age, petite, short hair, and wearing athletic clothes. I said to her, "Well, you look safe. I'll sit here."

She laughed, and I settled into the aisle seat. I was hoping to sleep for the duration of the flight, but for whatever reason, I felt wide awake. I looked her way from time to time and noticed that she was compiling a list of ministry donations she'd made. I assumed they were for tax purposes.

Only God could seat me next to a woman with a heart for ministries and the resources to help them, I thought. We eventually got around to introducing ourselves, and it turned out her name was Katie too. I told her I was an author and would like to give her a copy of my book. I pulled out a copy, and she shared that her brother, who was a priest, also wrote a book. We engaged in small talk, and Katie told me she lived on the east side of Milwaukee. When we landed, we wished each other well and exchanged business cards.

My trip in Tampa included ten days of fun in the sun. When it was time to head home, Katie and I found ourselves on the same return flight to Milwaukee. Although we did not sit together, God confirmed that he brought this woman into my life for a reason. I laughed inside and told him I had hoped it was for a big donation.

Fast forward a few weeks. A woman named Diane moved into Katie's neighborhood on the east side of Milwaukee and introduced herself as a new neighbor. Diane mentioned that she led the prison ministry at her local church, and Katie proceeded to tell Diane about meeting me on the airplane. A few days later, Diane visited the Milwaukee Women's Correctional Center to host her weekly Bible study, and an inmate told her about a book she was reading called *Call Me Vivian.*

Diane had enough experience with the Lord to know that her hearing about me was more than a coincidence, so she stepped out in faith and called me. When we talked, I shared more about my story and The Vivian Foundation. We met in person a short time later. I gave her a copy of my book and eventually provided hundreds of Christian books to her ministry.

It didn't take long for Diane to invite me to be a guest speaker at the Milwaukee Women's Correctional Center when they kicked off their new Bible study program. And to think that door opened because of the seat in which God placed me on an airplane. And he wasn't finished. God would eventually use Diane to endorse my book as a result of a letter she had sent to her team regarding my presentation style and our time together. She later opened the door to have my story featured in *Ring & Robe*, a publication for inmates. It proved to be the first of many speaking engagements at the facility in Milwaukee, and once again, God gets the glory for directing my steps and instructing others to step out in faith when prompted by the Holy Spirit to do so.

More and more letters from inmates poured in, touching my heart in unexpected ways. This was especially true with a letter and donation I received from a prisoner by the name of Alexander from Ellsworth, Kansas.

When I read that your ministry is dedicated to helping children of incarcerated parents and their families, I was instantly moved to do my best to give. I don't make but $21.00 a month, but that is a blessing if you ask me…I've told the Lord many times that it doesn't matter if I'm in prison or free from prison; I'll follow him and serve him.

Alex's donation was a true lesson in sacrificial giving, a lesson that can also be found in the Bible, when Jesus praised a poor widow for her generous giving. This was a stark contrast to the rich man whom Jesus taught us about in Mark 10:17–22.

As Jesus was starting out on his way to Jerusalem, a man came running up to him, knelt down, and asked, "Good Teacher, what must I do to inherit eternal life?"

"Why do you call me good?" Jesus asked. "Only God is truly good. But to answer your question, you know the commandments: 'You must not murder. You must not commit adultery. You must not steal. You must not testify falsely. You must not cheat anyone. Honor your father and mother.' "

"Teacher," the man replied. "I've obeyed all these commandments since I was young."

Looking at the man, Jesus felt genuine love for him. "There is still one thing you haven't done," he told him. "Go and sell all your possessions and give the money to the poor, and you will have treasure in heaven. Then come, follow me."

At this the man's face fell, and he went away sad, for he had many possessions.

The moral of this story was that this man loved riches more than he loved God; therefore, he broke the first and most important commandment: to love God above all else. What Jesus teaches us with this story is that our wealth can cause us to become self-reliant.

We tend to buy things when we feel empty, trying to fill a void that only God can fill. But even the person who has everything can still lack what is most important: eternal life.

God's Word tells us to whom much is given, much will be required, and God blesses us so we can bless others. One verse in Proverbs tells us that those who give to the poor are lending to the Lord (Proverbs 19:17), and this verse goes on to say and the Lord will pay you back. But those who trust in themselves will be humbled while those who depend on God will be blessed. James goes so far as to warn the rich in chapter 5: "This corroded treasure you have hoarded will testify against you on the day of judgment" (v. 3).

Here's the deal: You cannot "out give" God. God tells us in Malachi 3:10 that if we bring our tithes into the storehouse, then he will open the windows of heaven and "pour out a blessing so great you won't have enough room to take it in!" He goes on to say, "Try it! Put me to the test!" And whenever I see three exclamation points in a row in Scripture, I know God means business. Did you know that exclamation marks were originally called "notes of admiration"? And the word *admiration* means "a feeling of respect and approval."[14]

On the subject of blessings, God blessed me with twin grandsons! I was thrilled to become a grandma again. My three older grandsons were in high school, and it had been a long time since I had newborn babies to spoil. I could not help but think back to a time in prison when God revealed to me Zechariah 9:12: "Come back to the place of safety, all you prisoners who still have hope! I promise this very day that I will repay two blessings for each of your troubles."

Landon and Tyler entered this world together one day in early May. Landon weighed in at five pounds and thirteen ounces, and Tyler was only three ounces lighter than his slightly older brother. These boys were perfect in every way, and our family was so blessed to have welcomed them into the world. My daughter, Jenny, had worked full time until the boys' birth, and my son-in-law, Dan, was a teacher. We all expected a fun, busy summer helping them settle in to their new normal.

The twins garnished attention everywhere they went. They were fraternal, so it was fairly easy to tell them apart, but people are drawn to multiples in usual ways. Wherever they went, they became instant celebrities. Jenny returned to work for financial reasons, and she and Dan found a daycare option that, although expensive, would have been affordable.

When the boys were about six weeks old, Landon began experiencing trouble with keeping his bottle down. At first, it was sporadic, but it became progressively worse and developed into projectile vomiting. It sounded like a pyloric valve problem, which is not uncommon but requires surgery. With an afternoon doctor appointment scheduled, I sent a note asking my friends in Florida for prayer. Paula shared 1 Peter 2:24: "By his wounds you are healed," and she went on to write, "No surgery needed. Let's stand in agreement, sisters," and we did.

The doctor ordered an ultrasound for Landon, and the nurses were surprised when they saw how open his pyloric valve was. To quote Dan, "It looked like the parting of the Red Sea!" I forwarded the good news to my friends via text that all was well, and we would continue to monitor the situation with Landon. My friend Ruth Ann happened to be at a Bible study and did not receive my update until later that evening, but she was excited to tell me that the last prayer she prayed before heading to church that afternoon was, "Lord, if you could part the Red Sea, then you can heal Landon!" Trust me when I say that God had a hand in fixing that valve issue.

Two weeks later, I had a strange, vivid dream that left me wondering again what God was up to. In it, a very pregnant reindeer was living in our basement. I can't say I'd ever had a dream about a reindeer let alone one that was so pregnant it was ready to burst. I wondered if I might soon give birth to something exciting.

Given the peculiarity of this dream, I decided to do a little research on reindeer. They are interesting creatures known for many things besides transporting Santa Claus around the globe on Christmas Eve. I learned that reindeer represent loyalty, wisdom, resourcefulness, creativity, spirituality, journeying, wandering, safe travels, strength, and endurance. They are mobile, adaptable to new surroundings, and prefer freedom to keep moving. Reindeer also welcome opportunities to guide others in new directions.

With summer in full swing, I hated the thought of Jenny and Dan having to put my grandsons in daycare. They would be habitually sick from sharing close quarters with other kids, and my daughter would have to wake them up early, loading them in and out of a car during the freezing mornings of our unforgiving Wisconsin winters. Jenny and I were talking about childcare options, and she half-jokingly said, "Well, you're not doing anything. Maybe you should watch them." I laughed, dismissing the idea, but the longer I let it percolate in my heart, the more sense it made. I couldn't come up with a single good reason for Jenny and her family to go the route of daycare. God had revealed my next role, and Grandma Katie was not quite sure what to expect.

I agreed to provide full-time care for the boys, beginning in August, when both Jenny and Dan returned to work. I walked through their back door every weekday morning at 6:30, sometimes not walking out that same door until 6:30 in the evening, given Dan's coaching responsibilities. By June of the following year, I'd relinquished those duties after my daughter resigned from her customer service position to become a full-time stay-at-home mom.

Now I look back on that year that I spent with the boys and know it was by the grace of God that I managed to get through each day. I was learning and growing from the experience and quickly realized why patience is a virtue. If someone had told me that I would become a full-time babysitter of newborn twins in my sixties, I never would have believed them. God had certainly given me a "mulligan" to learn firsthand what I had missed with my own kids from working full time.

Each day was a new adventure that tested my strength and endurance. It helped that Landon and Tyler were happy babies. Naturally, they were on the same schedule, so when it came time for their bottles, I would put them in the twin pillow and feed them together. Of course, burping them quickly was not always easy, but they were cooperative for the most part. Many times, I'd hold them in my arms and feel so overcome by God's goodness that tears would well up in my eyes. Part of our daily ritual included sending a video or a photo to Jenny so that she could feel part of our day.

As the boys grew, I got my daily workout in Jenny and Dan's living room, where I routinely wore out the knees of my sweatpants. I was becoming a fan of *Sesame Street*, *Daniel Tiger's Neighborhood*, *Splash and Bubbles*, and *Dinosaur Train*. When they started becoming more mobile, particularly when they started standing without having any idea how to get back down, I wasn't sure I was going to make it. They figured it out eventually, and it wasn't long before they took their first steps, waddling around with their arms in the air like drunken sailors.

Their personalities really started to come out when they started to eat solid foods. Tyler's favorite was blueberries. He would pick through everything on his plate and devour them first. Landon, on the other hand, was more adventurous, eating virtually anything put in front of him.

They found their true passion, however, in books. From the day I started watching them to today, they loved to read. They had insatiable appetites for learning, and the day they clapped their hands in unison while I sang "If You're Happy and You Know It" was indeed special. I routinely made songs up, and one of our favorites was "We Are the Dancing Bears."

Of course, some days were challenging. It was always difficult to get Landon to fall asleep, and the smallest noise would wake him. I would usually try to put Tyler down before attempting to get Landon asleep. At one point, Tyler had a staph infection, and that was a long, long week. Then there was the day when their dog,

Maddy, ate a dirty diaper and had to be rushed to the vet's office. Still, I was mastering the fruit of the Spirit: love, joy, peace, patience, kindness, goodness, faithfulness, gentleness, and self-control in a season that, once again, I did not see coming.

It's been said that there's a reason why God gives you kids when you're young. Well, you know what? There are also many reasons why God gives you grandchildren when you're older. Grandchildren fill a place in your heart that you never knew was empty. There is no better love than the love of grandparents and great-grandparents, and my kids and grandkids have been blessed to experience both. When my kids were young, my grandparents came to our home each morning to babysit my children in much the same way. I came to appreciate their energy and subsequent exhaustion levels once I realized what they endured. And I, too, was able to sow into my grandsons in a way that I could not as a young mother to my kids.

Only God could have arranged that season of my life. I've never had so much fun, and I will forever cherish our memories together. God showed me how far I had truly come, and for the first time, I was able to pour true, godly love into others in the way that God has always intended. I was exactly where he needed me to be in order to prepare my heart for whatever was next. My heart was full, and my body was tired, but I knew Grandma Katie had made the most out of her God-given opportunity. It was time to move on to my next adventure.

1

I n early June, I headed to Redgranite Correctional Institution in central Wisconsin with my friend Mary Ann to visit her son, Dan, who was celebrating his fiftieth birthday. You may remember their story from *Call Me Vivian*, but I had been sitting next to Mary Ann on a flight from Tampa to Milwaukee, just days away from my sentencing hearing. Mary Ann was flying to Wisconsin to visit her family, including Dan, who was incarcerated at that time. God clearly instructed me to encourage her, and after two hours of conservation, God revealed to me that I would have a prison ministry.

As tradition had it, Mary Ann and I stopped for lunch at Schreiner's Restaurant on our way to visit Dan. Schreiner's is a throwback restaurant familiar to older people in Wisconsin. They serve fresh, home-cooked meals and irresistible desserts, and all of the servers wear white uniforms. The restaurant was fairly busy when we arrived. The host seated us in a middle booth, and as we settled in to make ourselves comfortable, our server greeted us. I did not catch her name, but her nametag said that she had been employed at Schreiner's for thirty-one years.

Mary Ann and I ordered their meatloaf, mashed potatoes, and a side salad. Our meal was delicious, and while our server tended to our needs, she casually asked us about our plans after lunch. We explained that we were on our way to prison for a visit, to which she replied with dead silence. It's not an unusual response to the mention of prison. She came back a second time, and I told her there was more to our story. She could hardly believe it when I told her that I had also spent time in prison and that I had met Mary Ann on an airplane when God seated the two of us together.

On her third visit to our table, our server's demeanor toward us had changed. She slid into the booth and shared how incarceration had affected her family. Her son served time in jail, having finished his sentence six years ago, and although it sounded like he was doing well, she talked about how difficult that time was as if it were yesterday. Feeling a prompting in my spirit, I returned to the car and grabbed a copy of *Call Me Vivian*. When I returned to our booth, I told our waitress that I wanted to give her a gift and explained a little bit more about *Call Me Vivian* and The Vivian Foundation. With tears in her eyes, she asked me to give her a hug. We hugged for what felt like an extended period of time, and she whispered, "You are one of God's angels."

God's presence overcame me in that moment, and I started to cry, and before long, Mary Ann was crying too. Reacting to the prompt in my spirit was a simple act of obedience to God, and yet it allowed me to bless another person in a powerful way.

Continuing to follow God's prompting, in July, I spent a good amount of time pouring over the information that Hannah, the former inmate who asked me to help her with her book, had provided about her life. I had already completed the prologue. Now my objective was to select the more powerful events of her life, particularly those from her childhood, so that I could help her write the opening chapters of her book.

For many of us, life as a kid was simple. We had an endless supply of energy and played outside all day with neighborhood friends. We explored everything. Our adventures took us up, down, and all around without hurry. Confident, we believed we could do anything. We laughed until our stomachs hurt, unafraid of failure. Our cheeks were rosy from living life to the fullest. Our lives were cheerful and carefree, and our most valuable gift was our ability to love unconditionally. We had this gift because we experienced Jesus with a pure heart.

What is a pure heart? Ask a child: "A pure heart means being kind. It's helping people, loving everyone, and putting others first." That's how my grandson Colin defined it when he was ten years old. His answer was enough to convince me that we should all look at life through the eyes of children.

Weeks before helping Hannah lay out her story, I had written a speech, "A Kid at Heart," for a ladies' luncheon at Hope Community Church. In hindsight, I realize that the timing of this speech paired with the timing of Hannah's story was hardly a coincidence. However, preparation for this luncheon led me to research a great deal about children, particularly childhood development.

As kids grow, their development progresses from total dependency on others to increased autonomy. It is a continuous process that follows a predictable sequence of events, and the child's experience of preceding events affects each developmental stage. In short, we behave the way we do because of what we've experienced: the good, the bad, and the ugly. We don't always understand why we act the way we do, but often, much of our behavior and many of our beliefs stem from our childhood influences.

One formative childhood influence is our birth order—that is, where we fall in our family's birth order can impact our personality.[15] For example, I was the firstborn child in my family, and it didn't take long for me to exhibit the classic traits of a firstborn child. Firstborn children usually garnish the most attention from their parents, enjoy a tremendous amount of one-on-one time, learn responsibility at a young age, and love the company of adults. We're inclined to agree with others and love to assume leadership roles, and although many are high achievers with an abundance of energy, firstborn children remain eager to please and continue to seek approval throughout their lifetime.

The behavioral traits of firstborns can be compliant, aggressive, or, as I found to be true, a combination of both. Because they are

natural leaders and often organized perfectionists driven to succeed, they don't allow much to stand in their way. Their confidence
is one reason why they enjoy the success that they do, but one of
their downfalls is their need to maintain an image of perfection. It's
why they often choose to hide their problems from others.

A second major influence on childhood development is positive reinforcement. Positive reinforcement improves children's
self-confidence and self-esteem. It allows youngsters to develop
self-reliance and independence, and it affirms that they are loved.
My earliest memories as a child date back to when I was four or
five, when I spent many Saturday mornings helping my grandma
clean. She would grab a silver, metal folding stool for me to stand
on and hand me a feather duster, and then I would reach as high as
I could to dust off the top of her hat boxes. She would tell me, "You
are such a big girl and so helpful! You are doing a wonderful job
helping me clean! Thank you!" This kind of positive reinforcement
from adults helped to positively shape my development. It affirmed
that I was good at something, that they appreciated me.

Childhood influences may go a long way, but we do not choose
when we are born, which family we are born into, or how many
siblings we have. We do not choose where we live, what our parents
do for a living, or where we go to school. We are products of our
environments, and some of those environments provide biblical
training and positive reinforcement while others do not. But I want
to let you in on a little secret. Regardless of where we find ourselves
in our family's birth order, how we were raised—with or without
positive reinforcement—or even how old we are today, we are still
God's children, and he has a great plan for each of us. Scripture
confirms this.

> You made all the delicate, inner parts of my body and knit
> me together in my mother's womb. Thank you for making
> me so wonderfully complex! Your workmanship is marvel-
> ous—how well I know it. You watched me as I was being

formed in utter seclusion, as I was woven together in the dark of a womb. You saw me before I was born. Every day of my life was recorded in your book. Every moment was laid out before a single day had passed. (Psalm 139:13–16)

God's character goes into the creation of every person. He knew you before you were born. He thought about you and planned for you long ago. You are extremely valuable in God's eyes: "Children are a gift from the LORD; they are a reward from him" (Psalm 127:3). You are not here by chance or accident. God created you as his forever friend.

As adults, we understand that a friend is a person we can trust. And a true friend stays by our side through good times and bad: "There are 'friends' who destroy each other, but a real friend sticks closer than a brother" (Proverbs 18:24). Friends listen to each other's problems, share encouraging words, and typically share similar attitudes, values, and interests. The depth and meaning found in friendships can be difficult to put into words.

Kids, on the other hand, have an entirely different perspective on friendship. For example, toddlers maintain friendship through affection, sharing, and play. It's not uncommon for a young child to approach another and simply ask, "Wanna be my friend?" Their love and acceptance of others is unconditional. As children mature, they become more aware of other kids and enjoy playing in groups.

It's been my observation throughout the years that once kids enter school, girls tend to make friends with other girls and boys tend to play with other boys. Girls tend to make friends as pairs whereas boys gravitate toward group play. The behaviors between boys and girls differ as well. While girlfriends are often busy exchanging secrets and playing with just one friend, boys tend to focus on games, action figures, and shared activities.

My childhood friends consisted of boys and girls who lived in our neighborhood, including my cousins. Our block had no shortage of kids. We spent many days playing kickball in the street or heading to Lakeview Park, where we would play on the swings, the merry-go-round, or the slide, or we'd play football or baseball for hours. Sports have always been an integral part of my life, and I was usually found in the driveway playing basketball.

My family lived a block away from the Racine Zoo, so it was not uncommon for us kids to head there for a freshly popped bag of popcorn, a snow cone, or cotton candy. We would check out the animals, pester the gorilla, make the lion roar, feed the ducks, and watch the otters dart around in the water. In the winter, we skated on the icy pond at the zoo and sat in the warming house until our feet thawed. We shared countless hours with our friends doing a variety of activities together, which is probably why these kinds of childhood friendships hold a special place in the hearts of many adults.

My childhood best friend was Jane. We shared common interests and always had fun together, although sometimes it was admittedly at the expense of others. Jane and her family lived in our neighborhood, and she and her sister, Nancy, were the youngest of six children. I was nine months older than Jane and one year ahead of her in school, but she stood a foot taller than me. We made a funny pair.

Jane's family was somewhat different from ours although that never seemed to matter. Whereas my dad was a schoolteacher, Jane's dad was an executive at a local publishing company. Her family had nicer clothes, a bigger house, expensive furniture, and catered dinner parties. Jane and I would hide under her family's dining room table during those parties, listening and watching everything and staying up much later than we were supposed to. They often invited me to join in their activities, and I considered myself blessed to experience things I otherwise would not have.

Jane's mom, Gloria, whom I remember as poised, sophisticated, and well dressed, would bring Jane and me to the North Shore Country Club. There, we swam in the Olympic-size pool, chased balls around the tennis courts, and bought whatever we wanted from the snack bar. I always felt special when they invited me to spend time at "the club." My mother was deathly afraid of water and passed her fear on to me, so I didn't know how to swim. Jane, on the other hand, was an accomplished swimmer, but she always hung out with me in the shallow end. If this annoyed or embarrassed her, she never let on to feeling that way. I even remember the day that I mustered the courage to jump off the high dive and into the deep end of the pool, where Jane waited for me. I'll never forget the relief I felt after finding my way to the side of the pool without drowning.

As kids, Jane and I were inseparable and spent a tremendous amount of time at each other's houses. That is, until Jane's mom received a breast cancer diagnosis. We had no clue what breast cancer meant, nor did we understand just how sick Gloria truly was. I remember her mother having to go to the Mayo Clinic, and I remember the day she died. It was Easter Sunday in 1968, and Jane was just ten years old. Gloria died on the same day that we celebrate Jesus' resurrection, and more than fifty years after her mother's passing, my heart still grieves for Jane and her family. To be honest, the impact of Gloria's passing did not fully hit me until I wrote this chapter. I simply cannot imagine *not* having a mom as a child.

For many of us, our mothers are, or once were, our best friends. Not only was my mom there for me and my siblings, but she also was there for Jane and her younger sister Nancy, who became integral members of our family. Jane has since shared with me that the unconditional love and encouraging words she received from my mom and dad helped her and Nancy; she doesn't know where life would have taken her had it not been for them.

Sadly, loss is a central experience for many children, and commonly, other family members or capable adults cannot step in and lend a helping hand and a loving heart. That's one of many reasons why it's so important to know Jesus. He promises that he will never leave us or forsake us (Hebrews 13:5). He is our ever-present helper and best friend. And when we feel alone, he is always, always with us. Nevertheless, parental separation, be it from death, divorce, incarceration, or removal to foster care, can have a major impact on a child's psychological development.

Unhappy childhood memories remain etched in the hearts and minds of many adults today. Some were forced to grow up in a hurry and missed out on what other children took for granted. Some were forgotten or uncared for; others suffered physical, verbal, or sexual abuse. Some lost their parents at an early age and never had a dad to play catch with or a mother to comfort them after skinning a knee. Other kids had parents with drug or alcohol addictions.

The children who grew up in these kinds of circumstances never went anywhere, nor could they invite friends over to play. They were too embarrassed or scared to talk about their struggles taking place at home. They struggled to survive. Some would just as soon forget about their childhood while others are grateful to have no recollection of what they endured.

All of these very real, very difficult childhood truths and experiences make the notion of becoming a kid at heart seem ridiculous, even impossible. But God desires that we exhibit childlike love and develop a childlike spirit of simple trust, joy, and ready laughter.

> The disciples came to Jesus and asked, "Who is the greatest in the Kingdom of Heaven?" Jesus called a little child to him and put the child among them. Then he said, "I tell you the truth, unless you turn from your sins and become like little children, you will never get into the Kingdom of Heaven. So anyone who becomes as humble as this little child is the greatest in the Kingdom of Heaven. And anyone who welcomes a little child like this on my behalf is welcoming me. (Matthew 18:1–5)

As wild as it may sound, my childlike spirit is exactly what got me through ten of the toughest years of my life, including the two years spent in federal prison. Regardless of my circumstances, I chose to have fun. I had childlike faith and believed in miracles, and throughout the process, I developed a childlike spirit of love.

If you read *Call Me Vivian*, then you know that a man, whom my family should have been able to trust, sexually abused me. God prepared my heart and directed the events in my life to confront the truth of that childhood trauma, but my willingness to process it with God was the key to my success. It was how God transformed my heart. In other words, my experience suggests that we sometimes must look back at what happened to us in order for our hearts to heal. We have to trust and obey God. It reminds me of the story of Abram.

Abram was called a "friend of God," and it's worth visiting a particular story from the book of Genesis about him and his obedience to the Lord.

> The LORD had said to Abram, "Leave your native country, your relatives and your father's family, and go to the land that I will show you. I will make you into a great nation. I will bless you and make you famous, and you will be a blessing to others. I will bless those who bless you and curse those who treat you with contempt. All of the families on earth will be blessed through you." (12:1–3)

Abram departed as the Lord instructed, and sometime later, the Lord spoke to Abram in a vision, telling him not to fear, for the Lord would protect him and reward him greatly. Abram longed to have children and shared this desire with the Lord, who brought him outside and said, "Look up into the sky and count the stars if you can. That's how many descendants you will have!" (15:5). In his heart, Abram believed the Lord, and "the LORD counted him as righteous because of his faith" (v. 6).

Sarai, Abram's wife, was convinced it was impossible for her to conceive given her age, so she encouraged Abram to have a child with a maid servant named Hagar. Although Sarai arranged for Hagar to have a child by Abram, she later blamed Abram for the results when Ishmael was born. But when Abram was ninety-nine years old, the Lord told him,

"Serve me faithfully and live a blameless life. I will make a covenant with you, by which I will guarantee to give you countless descendants...I will make you the father of a multitude of nations! What's more, I am changing your name. It will no longer be Abram. Instead, you will be called Abraham, for you will be the father of many nations. I will make you extremely fruitful. Your descendants will become many nations, and kings will be among them! I will confirm this covenant with you and your descendants after you, from generation to generation. This is the everlasting covenant: I will always be your God and the God of your descendants after you." (17: 1–7)

God also changed Sarai's name to Sarah and promised to bless her with a son. The Lord even told Abraham to name the baby Isaac. A year later, God kept his promise, and Sarah gave birth to Isaac. Years later, God tested Abraham's faith when he asked Abraham to sacrifice Isaac. Abraham, who had great faith, was confident that God would provide a substitute, and Abraham was right; God provided a ram to sacrifice instead (see Genesis 22). What God was truly asking of Abraham was to sacrifice Isaac in his heart to prove that Abraham loved God more than he loved his long-awaited son.

Just as God tested Abraham, God tests us to strengthen our character and deepen our commitment to him. Nothing that has happened to us is a surprise to God. Of course, it doesn't make those tests any less difficult or painful to experience, but through it all, we must remember that Jesus is our substitute, our ram. Whereas God stopped Abraham from sacrificing his son Isaac, God did not spare his own son, Jesus, from dying on the cross. If Jesus had lived, the rest of humankind would have died. But God sacrificed his one and only Son to die for us so that we would be spared from the eternal death that we deserve and instead live forever in heaven: "Everyone who believes in him will not perish but have eternal life. God sent his Son into the world not to judge the world, but to save the world through him" (John 3:16–17).

God has placed eternity in the human heart. And as a result, we will never be completely satisfied with earthly pleasures. It's why so many of us wonder what it is that we are supposed to be doing and think, *There's gotta be more to life than this!* That "more" that we continually seek can only be found in an intimate relationship with our heavenly Father. It's why we're created in his image. We have a spiritual thirst and eternal value, and nothing but an intimate relationship with God can truly satisfy us.

God's top priority for everyone is salvation. He specializes in changing hearts, and that's why it is important to understand the story of Nicodemus. Nicodemus was a Jewish religious leader and a Pharisee, and when he spoke to Jesus about his teachings and miraculous signs, Jesus taught him about becoming born again.

"No one can enter the Kingdom of God without being born of water and the Spirit. Humans can reproduce only human life, but the Holy Spirit gives birth to spiritual life. So don't be surprised when I say, 'You must be born again.' The wind blows wherever it wants. Just as you can hear the wind but can't tell where it comes from or where it is going, so you can't explain how people are born of the Spirit...

There is no judgment against anyone who believes in him. But anyone who does not believe in him has already been judged for not believing in God's one and only Son. And the judgment is based on this fact: God's light came into the world, but people loved the darkness more than the light, for their actions were evil. All who do evil hate the light and refuse to go near it for fear their sins will be exposed. But those who do what is right come to the light so others can see that they are doing what God wants." (John 3:5–8, 18–21)

As Jesus explained, we cannot control the work of the Holy Spirit, who plays a vital role in someone becoming a Christian. The Holy Spirit is a person, but we must remember that he is not simply any other person; he is God. We know the oneness of God the Father, God the Son, and God the Holy Spirit as the Trinity. Although this term is not found in the Bible, it's been used by the church over the ages to describe the truth found in Scripture. More simply, there is only one God, and he manifests and acts in three distinct persons.

The Holy Spirit works in the hearts of unbelievers to bring them to a place where they recognize their need for salvation. It is only then that, by the power of the Holy Spirit, someone can be born again. That's how we become a member of the body of Christ. Just as you did not control your physical birth, you cannot control your spiritual birth. It is a gift from God. He wants you to open the door of your heart so that he can transform your life, and your eternal destiny depends upon your decision to answer his call. If you are ready for a change of heart, pray one simple prayer: "Create in me a clean heart, O God. Renew a loyal spirit within me" (Psalm 51:10).

I want to close this chapter with an inspirational poem called "Children Learn What They Live" written by Dorothy Law Nolte.

If children live with criticism,
    they learn to condemn.
If children live with hostility,
    they learn to fight.
If children live with fear,
    they learn to be apprehensive.
If children live with pity,
    they learn to feel sorry for themselves.
If children live with ridicule,
    they learn to feel shy.
If children live with jealousy,
    they learn to feel envy.

If children live with shame,
  they learn to feel guilty.
If children live with encouragement,
  they learn confidence.
If children live with tolerance,
  they learn patience.
If children live with praise,
  they learn appreciation.
If children live with acceptance,
  they learn to love.
If children live with approval,
  they learn to like themselves.
If children live with recognition,
  they learn it is good to have a goal.
If children live with sharing,
  they learn generosity.
If children live with honesty,
  they learn truthfulness.
If children live with fairness,
  they learn justice.
If children live with kindness and consideration,
  they learn respect.
If children live with security,
  they learn to have faith in themselves
  and in those about them.
If children live with friendliness,
  they learn the world is a nice place in which to live.[16]

This poem captures the importance of leaving a positive impact on the lives of others. Our words have the power to tear people down or build them up, both of which can forever change a person's life. As the Bible says, "Don't use foul or abusive language. Let everything you say be good and helpful, so that your words will be an encouragement to those who hear them" (Ephesians 4:29).

8

A case manager from the Washington Corrections Center for Women in Gig Harbor, Washington, contacted me in September. He had read *Call Me Vivian*, so we talked about The Vivian Foundation and how it could provide resources to the facility, particularly their library named the Angel Network Library.

The Washington Corrections Center for Women opened in 1971 and is the largest women's prison in the state, housing more than seven hundred female inmates at various security levels. Their rehabilitation programs offer vocational and educational training and teach the women new skills that will help them transition into the outside world upon their release.

The case manager also set up a conversation between me and an inmate named Pamela, who was the Angel Network librarian. She, too, had read my book and excitedly told me about her position at the library, which she had held for almost three years. But it was time to pass her librarian duties on to another inmate.

"God knew exactly where I needed to be to strengthen my walk with him," Pamela said. "He walked me through the fire of losing my mom while here. I was placed in a position to spread his Word, to serve others, and to shine his light into the darkness. I am so humbled to be his trusted servant."

I was able to bless the Washington Corrections Center for Women with hundreds of books, along with journals, devotionals, and almost one thousand coloring books, all from BroadStreet

Publishing. The Vivian Foundation coloring booklet found its way into their visiting room too. Each woman in the facility's Residential Parenting Program, which allows pregnant, minimum-security inmates with sentences shorter than thirty months to keep their babies with them after giving birth, received a booklet to use with their other, older children during visits. Many inmates wrote letters to thank me for these resources, but God deserves the thanks and praise. He instructed me to develop the coloring booklet and operate a book ministry, and he moved their hearts to contact me. When you step out in faith, God always makes a way.

Another element of my ministry work is to provide godly counsel on a variety of subjects, and I often comfort people dealing with grief. Shortly after my work with the Washington Corrections Center for Women, my friend and former fellow inmate Christy called me. She was struggling to cope with the unexpected death of a family member and couldn't understand why it happened. It often feels like the people with the most admirable traits are the ones who leave this world too soon. Their kind souls, giving hearts, fun-loving personalities, and happy demeanors make it difficult for us to live without them.

Nevertheless, my conversation with Christy reminded me of a loss that I experienced during my incarceration. Six months into my sentence, an inmate at our compound unexpectedly died. The loss of her took place in June of 2012, and thankfully I felt compelled to document this experience in my journal at the time.

I had been facedown on the floor in my room giving praise to God with my friend and fellow inmate Susan. We were both so grateful for everything that God was doing in our lives. Another inmate from our unit, visibly upset, came into my room and told us, "Miss Mary was down in F3 and unresponsive."

Susan and I immediately stood up and went into the multipurpose room, where we could see the parking lot and a good portion of the compound. Through the large windows, we saw a rescue squad and a fire truck parked outside. The speed at which the medical staff moved gave away the severity of the situation. Susan, who was a nurse, ran to F3 to offer her assistance. We had never seen so many administrators on our compound at one time. Someone counted sixteen.

Chaplains arrived, and in short order, all of F3 was called to the visiting room. The remaining inmates were instructed to return to their units. In our hearts, we all understood what had happened although none of us wanted to speak it or believe it. F3 received the news first, and it did not take long for the rest of the compound to learn of Mary's passing.

It was close to eleven in the morning before the kitchen line servers were called to the cafeteria, almost an hour past our usual time. The air carried a quietness and sadness that's difficult to explain, and my spirit felt so heavy. The correctional officers called the F1, F2, and F4 units to lunch while the women of F3, still upset and grieving, remained in the visiting room. Most of the inmates had finished eating by the time F3 started to head toward the cafeteria. Mary's death visibly affected everyone—the officers, inmates, and administration. For the first time, we were one. United in our shared grief.

Town hall meetings were held in our individual units. There were tears and words of righteous indignation over the lack of medical care available to us. This sudden tragedy and loss caught us off guard, but how we responded was the important part. Thankfully, most everyone responded in love, knowing that God was in control. We prayed for Mary's family. We prayed for all of the women in her unit, and we prayed that we would be able to find the good that would come out of this tragedy.

I watched Mary's roommates return two bags of her bedding and clothing to the laundry. Others gathered her personal belongings in her room and at her workplace. By evening, we had erected a memorial for her in the F3 multipurpose room at the table where she routinely played Skip-Bo, her favorite card game. Everyone signed a sympathy card that was mailed to her family.

Our Women of Warfare Conference, originally scheduled for that afternoon, was moved to the evening so that more inmates could attend. The packed visiting room had an awesome night of Spirit-filled worship. As we sang the lyrics, "The Spirit of the Lord is here. I feel it in the atmosphere," I began to pray in my prayer language and told God that I wanted to carry this story to the world.

Two days after Mary's passing, a memorial service was held in her honor. It would be the first funeral I'd attend in prison. The skies opened up, and rain hit the ground. It appeared and felt as though tears were falling from heaven. I thought of Jeremiah 9:17–18: "Call for the mourners. Send for the women who mourn at funerals. Quick! Begin your weeping! Let the tears flow from your eyes." Given the somberness on the compound, I knew in my heart that it was going to be a difficult evening.

Eventually, the rain stopped, and the sun began to peek through the clouds. I waited to enter the memorial service until the procession of inmates from F3 ended. The inmates from her unit entered hand in hand, two by two. Each wore their green uniform pants and either a white or gray t-shirt with a black ribbon pinned to it in honor of Mary. Ushers dressed in white escorted them to seats.

F3 sat on the left side of the room while inmates from the other three units sat on the right. Palm leaves decorated both the front and back of the room, and "It Is Well with My Soul" played in the background as we entered. There was a picture of Mary, too, accompanied with the words, "Gone but not forgotten." A second sign contained Scripture from John 11:25: "I am the resurrection and the life." As I took my seat in the last row, I immediately felt God's presence.

The service began with a speech from the associate warden, who called Mary "a strong woman of God." He spoke about the influence that people have on your life. Mary touched many lives at Coleman, and it was obvious that her impact continued beyond her death. I learned that Mary was born in 1950, and prison had been her home for over sixteen years. She had received a twenty-five-year sentence and had seven years left to serve in prison after receiving a reduced sentence for good behavior.

Although I didn't know Mary well, she wore her emotions where I could see them. Each day that she proceeded through the serving line, she looked dejected. As sad as it is, I never saw her smile. Looking down at my prison boots, I wiped away a tear and wondered how many more individuals would have to endure what Mary did. My heart hurt, which told me that the Holy Spirit was also grieving.

The service continued with praise and worship, and Mary's closest friends spoke about their relationships with "Miss Mary."

"We weren't just friends," one said. "We were family."

Only inmates can truly know what that means during incarceration. For some, their fellow inmates are the only family they have ever truly known. Another friend of Mary's, who was in her seventies, sang a song and received a standing ovation; one woman read a poem, and others shared so many funny stories. Mary was remembered as compassionate and kind, always wishing everyone a good morning.

Mary was known for saying, "If you have a problem, get mad, cry, and get over it!" That sounded much too easy. Many women saw themselves in Mary, and yet others saw Mary in those they love. Mary's best friend at Coleman, Miss Cook, could not even bring herself to attend the service.

Wanda, someone I worked with and a member of my kitchen family, stepped up to the podium, heartbroken. She was quiet but had a comedic side to her. She liked to make us laugh and was always joking around with the guards. She was a hard worker, quick to lend a helping hand. Wanda stood in tears at the podium for close to a minute; it took everything she had to collect herself and muster the strength and courage to speak. I was about to encounter a side of Wanda that I had never met.

First, Wanda talked about how prison had affected her own family. Many of her family members had faced convictions for drug charges. Wanda's grandmother, for example, had received a twenty-four-year sentence and died in prison without Wanda having a chance to say goodbye. Her aunt received a thirty-three-year sentence, her cousin seventeen years, and her uncle received life in prison. Wanda sobbed uncontrollably as she said, "I have never told anyone the length of my sentence. I received sixteen and a half years." She kept crying and repeated over and over again, "We are good people. We are good people."

Wanda's speech left me in tears like most everyone else. Mary had been like a grandmother to Wanda. Her death brought up every painful emotion that Wanda had tried to suppress over the last seven years of her incarceration, finally allowing Wanda a space to release the pain of not saying goodbye to her actual grandmother. Wanda could let go of the shame and anger that she had held on to—over her charges, the length of her sentence, and the impact these crimes had on her family. Wanda had just touched hundreds of lives, including mine. I wiped away my tears, knowing that God was once again working this situation for good and helping Wanda begin to heal her heart.

The next speaker was one of Mary's coworkers, who found a note in Mary's desk dated two years earlier. The word *repent* and the phrase "70 x 7" was written on the top of the page followed by a list of Bible verses that told us a little bit more about what Mary valued and what we should consider important.

"Those who love their life in this world will lose it. Those who care nothing of their life in this world will keep it for eternity. Anyone who wants to serve me must follow me, because my servants must be where I am. And the Father will honor anyone who serves me." (John 12:25–26)

Only fools say in their hearts, "There is no God." They are corrupt, and their actions are evil; not one of them does good! The LORD looks down from heaven on the entire human race; he looks to see if anyone is truly wise, if anyone seeks God. But no, all have turned away; all have become corrupt. No one does good, not a single one! Will those who do evil never learn? (Psalm 14:1–4)

Mary also loved Mark chapter 7. It teaches about inner purity, faith, and healing, and 2 Corinthians 5:21 was her signature verse and parting message to those she loved: "For God made Christ, who never sinned, to be the offering for our sin, so that we could be made right with God through Christ."

Mary was a born-again Christian, and we all took comfort in knowing that Jesus ushered her into her heavenly home. What I did not realize was that given Mary's declining health, she had applied for a compassionate release and was awaiting a decision on her application. It was God, however, who ultimately set her free, and Mary would finally be reunited with her three children who predeceased her, two of whom, I was told, had died in prison.

I had another experience to minister on grief and loss while I was at Coleman. Crystal was in my unit and had already been in prison for six years on drug charges when I met her. She couldn't wait to return home and show everyone in her life the positive changes she had made. She was particularly excited for her ex-boyfriend, who was also her daughter's father, to see her transformation. They hadn't spoken in years given his anger toward Crystal and her incarceration, but she decided to step out in faith and call him. He answered, which Crystal considered a gift from God.

"I thought I was dreaming because all of his anger was gone!" she told me. She ended up calling him a second time that evening and again the next day.

Crystal shared more about the situation with her ex-boyfriend with me, and she aired thoughts and feelings that she had clearly locked inside her heart for a long time. I shared Scripture with her on the importance of forgiving others and encouraged her to thank God for softening her ex's heart. We were thrilled for how things were working out between them, and it was obvious that Crystal's heart was experiencing major healing.

Just three days after our initial discussion, as I sat outside waiting to go to work, Crystal approached me with tears in her eyes.

"Katie," she started. "I need to tell you that my daughter's dad died…the ex-boyfriend that I told you about. I can't believe what God was able to do this week to make things right between us, and I just wanted to tell you that."

"I'm so sorry, Crystal," I told her. I went on to remind her that God is faithful and had bestowed a wonderful gift to the two of them by restoring their relationship.

In the days, weeks, and months that passed after the loss of her former boyfriend, Crystal remained a pillar of strength, teaching others about the gift of forgiveness, giving God the glory whenever she shared her miraculous testimony.

We all have a story. I have heard stories riddled with heartache and pain; others filled with violence and abuse, and still more of hopelessness and regret. God uses tough, painful experiences to conform us to his image and to win our hearts, and sometimes that tough, painful experience is death. God cares deeply every time one of his loved ones dies, and he promises to work all things for good (Romans 8:28). Take Mary's death for example. Her passing showed me how death can draw people together and facilitate healing. The death of Crystal's ex-boyfriend showed me that forgiveness is not only a choice but also a precious gift.

No matter our story, our journey here on earth has always been about God, whose spirit is ready to work in us. Each day he gives us opportunities to better exhibit Christlike behaviors of love, joy, peace, patience, kindness, goodness, faithfulness, gentleness, and self-control. And whenever I encounter people grappling with grief, I direct them to Psalm 139:16: "You saw me before I was born. Every day of my life was recorded in your book. Every moment was laid out before a single day had passed." We cannot add one day to our life; that's why we must try to live each day to its fullest.

9

cottie Barnes of Forgiven Ministry was in Raleigh when she called me, overcome with emotion as she left the North Carolina Correctional Institution for Women (NCCIW). I was scheduled to speak at this same facility the following week for Forgiven Ministry's "One Day with God" event, a two-day camp reuniting incarcerated parents with their children.

"I have never seen a book like *Call Me Vivian* so highly requested by inmates and staff, Katie," Scottie said. "I can't wait for you to meet all of these ladies. God is doing amazing things with your testimony. We're so excited for your visit."

Forgiven Ministry's mission is to meet the spiritual, physical, and emotional needs of current and former inmates, their children, and their families by showing the love of Christ in a tangible way. One of those ways is through their "One Day with God" camps, and forty women at NCCIW had earned the privilege to attend camp that year because of their good behavior.

As I waited inside the Milwaukee airport to board my flight to Raleigh, God clearly told me, *It is time to be bold!* His command prompted me to open my Bible and turn to Joshua 1:9, which happened to be the same Scripture God had given me when I was airlifted to the county jail in Chickasaw, Oklahoma, in 2013 to testify in the trial of the last defendant in the case with which I was involved. Joshua 1:9 reads, "This is my command—be strong and courageous! Do not be afraid or discouraged. For the LORD your

God is with you wherever you go." But nothing could have prepared me for what I would experience at "One Day with God."

This was my first visit to Raleigh, and I secretly hoped I would have enough time to visit Durham and Chapel Hill, mere miles away, to soak in the Duke–North Carolina basketball rivalry I'd come to love. Scottie and her husband, Jack, picked me up at the airport, and to my delight and surprise, the chaplain of NCCIW stepped out of the vehicle to greet me too. I felt like a celebrity! We all exchanged hugs before driving to West South Street, where we approached the front doors to the home of Robert and Deborah Nash, our host family for the weekend. Staying with them would be Scottie, Jack, a woman who was also a volunteer, and myself. The Nash's brick home, built in 1935, featured an inviting front porch and stunning interior design. The couple had lived there for years and welcomed us with such warmth. They woke up early to prepare coffee and breakfast for us, generously meeting every one of our needs. They even introduced me to toasted Asiago cheese bread with butter and homemade jam (I still think of them whenever I enjoy Asiago bread!). God had clearly blessed the Nash family with the spiritual gift of serving, loving hearts because I immediately felt at home.

With a full schedule ahead of us on Friday and Saturday, I turned in early that Thursday evening, hoping for a restful night of sleep. I ended up tossing and turning all night though—too excited with the anticipation of what God had planned.

The number of volunteers needed to host an event like this required assistance from a local church. Christ Our King Community Church, located near the prison, would help transport volunteers and children to the facility while caregivers remained at the church. But since the children would not arrive until Saturday morning, that meant Friday's focus would be on the mothers.

We pulled into the prison's parking lot on Friday morning just before seven. The early start gave us extra time to check in and set everything up prior to the mothers' arrival at nine. We passed through metal detectors, and then a guard escorted us to the gymnasium where the event would take place. I realized we'd be on a basketball court and had to smile. "One Day with God" was one of the biggest events in which I'd participated to date, and only God could have orchestrated it to unfold inside a gym, lining me up next to other speakers who shared my passion for the game.

When it comes to sports, basketball was my first love even though I was technically a better softball player. Way back in 1975, when I was a senior at Saint Catherine's High School in Racine, our team played in Wisconsin's first ever Independent Schools Athletic Association State Basketball Championship game, which also happened to be the first state championship ever held for girls. As captain of the team and starting guard, I had such high hopes for us. Sadly, we lost by three points and finished the season as the state's runner-up. I was the only senior on the team, which meant I was the only one who wouldn't get a second chance to win it all the next year. I took the loss hard.

Sure enough, the very next season, my former team went undefeated and won the coveted Gold Ball. I sat in the bleachers and watched them celebrate their victory. I was genuinely happy for them, but I struggled hard with it internally. I asked the same question over and over in my head: *Why was I the only one who didn't get a second chance?* I honestly did not come to grips with that heartbreaking loss for years, but it didn't extinguish my love for the game either. March Madness remains my favorite time of the year, and I've had the privilege to attend both the men's and women's Final Four Championship games. Nevertheless, that Friday morning, as I stood on a basketball court inside the largest state prison in North Carolina, I understood why I had to wait for my second chance; it had manifested itself in a way that I never could have imagined.

Temperatures hovered near ninety degrees, so the gymnasium's windows were open, and large fans circulated copious amounts of hot air around us. I was confident in my ability to share my testimony, but between the heat and my long pants and T-shirt, one thing was certain: I was going to have to lean on God for the strength to get through the weekend.

Forty women entered the gym, and I felt an immediate pull toward each one of them. Common prison protocol required a head count when they arrived, and it brought back memories of my own time in prison that I had somehow managed to suppress since my release; I almost instinctively jumped in line with them. Some things you never forget.

The inmates and volunteers formed a big circle in the gym to open the day with prayer. The inmates formed a semicircle on one side, and the volunteers formed a complementary configuration directly across from them. A prompting in my spirit led me to jog to the inmates' side. The chaplain led the prayer, and I was so overcome with God's presence that all I could do was cry. Everything that God had promised throughout this journey was playing out right before my eyes, and quite honestly, it was overwhelming.

As the schedule and agenda dictated, I remained in the gymnasium with the women during praise and worship. While other presenters facilitated the inmates' preparation time with Scripture study, Scottie and I headed to the Robbins Unit to visit other inmates. The Robbins Unit housed two infirmaries, both of which we would visit. Many of these women had received copies of *Call Me Vivian* ahead of time and were looking forward to meeting me and having their books signed. Whenever I'm asked to sign a book, I feel overwhelmed in the best way possible. It's joyful and flattering, of course, but those moments also remind me that God is using my testimony—and me. It's a powerful reminder that I am valued in the kingdom of heaven.

The elevator door slid open, and the sight of inmates resting in hospital beds, locked inside cells, caught me off guard, and something shifted deep inside my soul. I felt as though I were seeing their circumstances through the eyes of Jesus. I no longer saw inmates; I simply saw women of all races, ethnicities, sizes, and shapes as one. God was showing me that these were his sick and wounded lambs who desperately needed love. His presence reminded me of 1 Samuel 16:7: "The LORD doesn't see things the way you see them. People judge by outward appearance, but the LORD looks at the heart." It also reminded me of the time during my incarceration when God told me, *This journey has never been about who was right or wrong; this journey has always been about your heart.*

One by one, I greeted each woman individually, offering a hug or handshake. I listened to their stories, however brief, and told each of them that God loves them. Some were unable to leave their rooms, in which case I approached their doorways to make each woman feel special and encourage her. We also left behind small gifts from The Vivian Foundation, and for a short time, I truly believed these women forgot where they were. Two ladies from an organization called Dribble for Destiny had accompanied us to the infirmary and displayed their basketball-handling abilities. We played games with inmates who were able to participate, and their laughs and smiles were priceless. We prepared to leave, and an inmate asked if she could pray for me.

"Of course," I replied.

"God," she started, "I ask in the mighty name of Jesus that you take Katie's book to all of the ends of the earth for your glory. Amen."

Not only her kindness but also the kindness of everyone else touched me. We were off to the next unit, where we repeated the same activities. God even allowed me to minister to some of the staff members who had read my book and waited to meet me. Scottie had been right; the Lord *was* doing amazing things with my testimony. After exiting the second infirmary, Scottie pulled me aside as we walked along the sidewalk toward another building.

"We have one more place to visit before heading back to our event," Scottie said. "Katie, it's time to visit death row."

When I least expected it, God had opened the door for me to minister to women who, as a result of their crimes, were sentenced to death. Scottie had visited these ladies before, but this was my first time. According to the Death Penalty Information Center, "around 2,500 prisoners currently face execution in the United States."[17] We don't hear much about executions, but at least one is scheduled every month. Lethal injection is most commonly used, but other methods are authorized as well. Trust me when I tell you that nothing can prepare you for a visit like this.

I took a deep breath before walking toward the elevator and heading upstairs. Two guards sat at their command post, expecting our arrival. After completing proper security protocol, the first steel door opened and closed behind us and then a second one. Then I stepped inside a space that few people ever experience.

Dressed in maroon jumpsuits and awaiting our arrival were all three death row inmates: Blanche, Carlette, and Christina. Blanche, also known as "the Black Widow," was in her mid-eighties and the oldest among them. She had been on death row since November of 1990 and was convicted of murdering one of her husbands and a boyfriend by slipping arsenic into their food. She's suspected of having killed others in the same manner. Given her death sentence, she never faced trial for the other murders or the attempted murder of another husband.

Carlette was in her fifties and a former home health care worker. The facility had received Carlette on April 1, 1999, after she had kidnapped an eighty-six-year-old woman, forced her to withdraw money from her bank account, and then murdered her. At the time of the woman's murder, Carlette was thirty-four years old. The youngest death row inmate, Christina, was in her late thirties and had been on death row since July of 2000. A member of a local gang, Christina kidnapped and murdered two women at random as part of her gang initiation. A third victim had been left for dead but survived the attack.

My eyes cautiously looked beyond the spot where we stood in order to survey the women's living quarters: seven cells, a common area used for eating and visiting, and a small, secure concrete patio that the inmates were permitted to use for one hour each day. What

I found particularly interesting was their view, which overlooked the prison's chapel. I paused. Jesus was confirming to me once again that, regardless of their crimes, I had to see these women through his eyes. As 1 John 1:8–9 reads, "If we claim we have no sin, we are only fooling ourselves and not living in the truth. But if we confess our sins to him, he is faithful and just to forgive us our sins and to cleanse us from all wickedness."

We spent a fair amount of time visiting, and each woman received a copy of *Call Me Vivian*. They showed me their handiwork, as they had all learned to crochet and spent a fair amount of time crafting. It brought me back to my time at Coleman and reminded me of the artistic talent of so many of the inmates there too. I wondered if these women had missed their calling. It was clear that we all enjoyed our time together, and all too soon, it was time to say goodbye. I enjoyed a long embrace with Blanche, then Christina, and finally Carlette, who sobbed in my arms and told me she did not think she could endure another day.

While exiting through the same set of steel doors through which we entered, I thanked God for this opportunity. Given the state of my heart at that moment, I understood that the Lord had brought me to another level of my ministry call. I let out a deep sigh as we left that part of the facility, grateful and humbled that he had chosen me for such an assignment.

Scottie and I returned to the gymnasium and grabbed sandwiches for lunch. Meanwhile, the inmates were busy making crafts and preparing gift bags for their children. They all wore their bright green "One Day with God" shirts. Volunteers performed a ceremony called "the Crowning of the Mothers," during which each mother received a tiara and listened to volunteers reiterate how special they are. Self-esteem and confidence are often greatly lacking among inmates considering their circumstances, so it was important to boost their morale and lift their spirits, which would hopefully carry over into the following day. A guest singer entertained the women, and Forgiven Ministry showed a powerful video captured by ABC's *Nightline* from a "One Day with God" camp that had taken place at another facility to help prepare the women for what to expect on Saturday.

The time came for me speak, and I was allotted forty-five minutes to share my testimony. I made sure to share a video from Candice Glover's award-winning performance on *American Idol* in 2012, when she sang, "When You Believe." I had watched that season finale while incarcerated at Coleman, and I knew that evening, as I sat in federal prison, that everything God had promised would come true. As the video started and Candice's voice rang out through the gymnasium, my emotions flooded through me once again. The lyrics were so timely, and my life is proof that miracles truly can happen when you believe. I finished my afternoon speech, but I could sense that it lacked something. I asked the volunteers for candid feedback and made revisions for my evening speech, which would be in front of even more inmates.

We ate a quick dinner before the officers opened the doors to the gym, and more than one hundred fifty inmates came to hear my story. Each attendee received a Bible reading plan and a copy of *Call Me Vivian*. Although I had revised my evening speech, I closed my portfolio when I reached the podium and told God, *This is your show. You are going to have to take over because I'm running on empty.*

For the next hour, the inmates laughed and cried as the Holy Spirit spoke through me. I cannot even tell you what I said because they were not my words but truly the words of God. I handed off the microphone to the gals from Dribble for Destiny. Hugs and high fives abounded afterward, and the volunteers told me they, too, were moved by what they had witnessed. Nearly one hundred women gave their lives to Christ that night, and I knew I was exactly where I was supposed to be. Exhausted, Scottie, Jack, and I headed back to the Nash's home. I had never felt so spiritually, emotionally, and physically drained in my life.

Saturday morning was another early wakeup call. It was a warm, sunny day in Raleigh, and with temperatures in the eighties and even more bodies inside the gymnasium, it was certain to be another hot one. Instead of heading directly to the prison, we first headed to the church to greet the children.

As kids arrived and settled in, I met Sandra Kearns from On Wings Like a Dove Ministry. Her ministry partners with Forgiven Ministry to distribute to the children treasure boxes filled with coloring books, crayons, word search puzzles, and other activities. Caregivers received giftbags too. Some of the kids enjoyed the snacks we had set out while others had their faces painted. Some of the kids were outgoing and quick to share about themselves. Others were more introspective, and you could see the apprehension lined on their faces. Believe it or not, some children meet their mother or father for the first time through "One Day with God" camps. Regardless, we all made sure to be patient and supportive as they adjusted.

We needed to board the bus and leave the church at nine o'clock in order to allow enough time for the children to be processed at the prison. Caregivers had to remain at the church, as security concerns prohibited them from entering the prison. Once each child was successfully processed, they entered the waiting room with their designated volunteer. Unlike the other volunteers, my assignment did not involve working with a child. I would participate in the morning events, but in the afternoon, I would return to the church to speak to the caregivers and then travel back to the prison toward the end of the program to say goodbye.

After the children were processed, volunteers escorted them to the gymnasium, which meant they had to walk across the compound and past other inmates. The kids had full visibility of the prison surroundings, and I wondered what thoughts crossed their minds. I hoped and prayed they were focused on one thing: reuniting with their mothers.

The music began, and the mothers stood at the baseline on one side of the basketball court. One by one, as their children's names were announced, the child entered through the double doors of the gym and ran the length of the floor into their mother's arms. The clapping that ensued with the announcement of each name continued until each child and mother had their time to shine. Many mothers welcomed more than one child into their arms, leaving them tangled up in a pile on the floor together, all wrapped up in one big mama-bear hug. The joy inside that gym was tangible and a feeling that I will never forget. I even ran out of tissues before all of the children had reunited with their mothers.

One of the most painful parts of the day, however, was having to tell one of the mothers that her child was unable to attend. We did not know why. She began to break down, and I felt a tug in my heart to go over to her, take her in my arms, and hold her tightly, comforting her as best I could. I held her face in my hands and looked at her red-rimmed eyes, telling her that we had to trust God even though it hurt and we had no answer or explanation. We do not know the Lord's thoughts or understand his plans, but we do know that God works all things for good (Micah 4:12; Romans 8:28).

The decibels in the gym were rising with the temperature and the excitement, and it was time for the fun and games to begin. Dribble for Destiny entertained the families with basketball relay games. Everyone celebrated missed birthdays with cake and a booming rendition of "Happy Birthday." While the inmates were busy enjoying time with their children, Scottie introduced me to Patricia, a woman Scottie had previously told me about.

Patricia had been on death row for more than twenty-five years for murdering her husband, and through an appeal, the court commuted her sentence to life in prison. That ruling meant that she could remain with the general population rather than the death row inmates, but she would never be released from prison. What Scottie had initially told me about Patricia was that *Be Still and Know*, a coloring book from BroadStreet Publishing that The

Vivian Foundation had donated to the facility, had saved Patricia's life. When I met Patricia at "One Day with God," I asked if she felt comfortable sharing her experience with me, and she was happy to oblige.

I stood at the officer's station, waiting for my signature on my work sheet. An officer had placed her mug on the counter and started yelling at me to get away from her coffee.

"I'm not touching it," I said.

She shouted back, "But you are breathing."

I told her I wish I wasn't. I returned to my laundry room job, thinking of all the reasons why I'd be better off dead. The seed of suicide had been planted.

Over the next four months, I sought counseling from a mental health professional and kept my weekly appointments, but the seed grew into an obsession. I felt useless to God, myself, and others. There was no hope or future, and I was helpless to change it. I withdrew from all religious activities, and my eating, sleeping, and social habits changed. I just wanted to be alone. Thoughts of suicide prevailed over everything that required my attention: conversation, reading, TV. I identified with Jonah in the belly of the fish: "I went down to the bottom of the mountains" (Jonah 2:6 GNT). You can't get deeper and darker than that.

I had my plan, set a date, gave away my possessions, wrote a note, and was counting down the days of my final week when I decided to ask the chaplain about the theological consequences of suicide. She insisted on seeing me the next day and every day that week. When she gave me a coloring book and pencils, I thought, *Thanks, but I have no intention of returning to a childhood pastime.* Still, I paged through it, and Psalm 22:19 caught my attention: "LORD, do not be far from me. You are my strength, come quickly to help me" [NIV]. I realized I had not called on God.

I began coloring and rereading Scripture. After a while, I realized I wasn't thinking about death but about what color I should use next. In the following days, I would color whenever suicidal thoughts invaded. And the more complicated and detailed the picture was, the more I concentrated on it. My "date" passed, and I'm still here.

Because of Patricia's story and with God's help, over seventeen hundred inmates at NCCIW were blessed with coloring books compliments of BroadStreet Publishing, The Vivian Foundation, and Forgiven Ministry, Inc. About a month after "One Day with God," Patricia sent me a letter telling me that she had started her own ministry inside the walls of the prison and had helped four other inmates who were battling suicidal thoughts. And instead of waking up in tears from feelings of hopelessness, Patricia woke up in tears over the awesomeness of God.

As "One Day with God" came to a close, I stood outside the prison gate, watching the mothers and their children release balloons into the sky. It was their last activity together before saying goodbye and returning to the caregivers waiting in the prison parking lot. I watched as every child, regardless of their age, fell into the arms of their trusted caregivers, sobbing over having to say goodbye to their mothers. My heart swelled with compassion in a way I had never experienced before. Tears rolled down my cheeks, and I thanked God for allowing me to be a part of the event.

That weekend taught me a powerful, intense lesson in compassion and empathy. Most of us liken empathy to putting ourselves in someone else's shoes, and in my case, I *had* worn those women's shoes. I understood their feelings and identified with them all too well. The thing is, though, that empathy doesn't always look the same. Psychologists define three types of empathy: cognitive, emotional, and compassionate. Cognitive empathy is the ability to put yourself in someone's position and see matters from their perspective. It's "empathy by thought" rather than feeling. "Emotional empathy is when you quite literally feel the other person's emotions alongside them." It's good because it means that you "readily understand and feel other people's emotions," but it can also become overwhelming. Compassionate empathy is when we feel someone's pain and take action to help, and that's what ministry work is all about.[18]

First Peter 3:8 says we are to all be of one mind, and that one mind that Peter is referring to is the mind of Christ. According to Peter, oneness is created by treating one another with compassion, love, tenderness, and courtesy—four qualities that lie at the heart of empathy. That's why we must develop a deep understanding of who people are, how they became that person, what they know, how they learned it, how they feel, and why they feel that way.

We are all sinners saved by God's grace because we have all fallen short of God's glorious standard. David committed adultery. Moses murdered an Egyptian. Saul, who later became Paul, killed Christians, including those closest to Jesus. Peter denied even knowing Jesus, and Rahab was a prostitute. Jonah ran from God, and Matthew was despised. God uses our failures, hardships, and trials for his glory.

> Dear brothers and sisters, when troubles of any kind come your way, consider it an opportunity for great joy. For you know that when your faith is tested, your endurance has a chance to grow. So let it grow, for when your endurance is fully developed, you will be perfect and complete, needing nothing. (James 1:2–4)

Notice that James does not say *if* trouble comes your way; he says *when* trouble comes your way. We cannot know the depth of our character until we face hardships. And if our hearts remain open, we may even find our true purpose in life.

10

In March of 2018, BroadStreet Publishing emailed me with exciting news. If you recall, just a few months earlier, they had donated to The Vivian Foundation more than six thousand books, which were shipped to Forgiven Ministry and the Prison Book Project. So when BroadStreet told me that they were gifting The Vivian Foundation another forty-five thousand books, my jaw dropped. While I was grateful to receive the donation, I reread the email and thought, *What in the world am I going to do with forty-five thousand books?*

In less than one week, I found a home for every. Single. Book. Twenty-five thousand coloring books arrived at prisons in North Carolina, Michigan, New Mexico, and Texas. We blessed out-of-state halfway houses with Christian resources and delivered a full truck-load of books to the Salvation Army of Southeastern Wisconsin. Locally, we supplied resources to Youth for Christ; Teen Reach Adventure Camps; Faith, Hope, and Love for Kids; Community Policing Houses; and a number of local churches, nursing homes, and high schools. God was opening doors far beyond the scope of anything I could have imagined. Within a few short months, we were able to bless both local and national organizations with retail inventory valued over one million dollars! As the adage goes, those who put everything in God's hands will eventually see God's hands in everything.

I received a beautiful card from Patricia at NCCIW adorned with Romans 8:38: "Nothing can ever separate us from God's love." Patricia also penned a note.

> My therapist gave me an assignment…She said, "Since you seem to have a spiritual connection with Vivian (that's what she calls you), I want you to write her a letter…Let her know exactly what your thoughts are and what is really going on in your life, but you don't have to mail it."…If I do it, don't worry, I won't mail it. Besides, how can I write something I don't even understand myself?

This was definitely a God thing. That very day I mailed a card to Patricia, encouraging her to complete the assignment because I had a powerful prompting in my spirit to do the same for her.

How do we explain spiritual connections with others? I had only met Patricia a few months prior. I knew God's Word would provide the answer, so I sat down at my computer and asked the Holy Spirit to guide me through Scripture. The message that kept resonating in my spirit? Kindness is perfect love.

The Bible clearly tells us that God is love: "Let us continue to love one another, for love comes from God. Anyone who loves is a child of God and knows God. But anyone who does not love does not know God, for God is love" (1 John 4:7–8). First Corinthians 13:4–7 assigns fifteen attributes to love.

> Love is patient and kind. Love is not jealous or boastful or proud or rude. It does not demand its own way. It is not irritable, and it keeps no record of being wronged. It does not rejoice about injustice, but rejoices whenever the truth wins out. Love never gives up, never loses faith, is always hopeful, and endures through every circumstance.

Then God directed me to another familiar Scripture: "My thoughts are nothing like your thoughts…and my ways are far beyond anything you could imagine" (Isaiah 55:8). I never imagined getting caught up in a workplace romance that turned criminal or spending two years in federal prison as result. I never imagined writing a book and distributing it into three thousand jails and prisons across the United States. I never imagined starting a nonprofit organization dedicated to helping families of the incarcerated, donating more than one hundred thousand Christian books, twenty-five thousand Bible reading plans, ten thousand "Heaven Cent" poems, ten thousand "Pass It On" cards, and ten thousand coloring booklets. I never imagined ministering to women on death row. Meeting Patricia was all part of God's perfect plan for both of our lives.

The Lord's purpose for us on this earthly journey is simple: God wants us to have an intimate relationship with his Son, Jesus Christ, and to serve others in love. To believe in God means to put our trust, confidence, and faith in Jesus because he is the only one who can save us. We must surrender our will and put Jesus Christ in charge of our earthly life and eternal destiny. We must also believe that God's Word is true and reliable.

When you ask Jesus into your heart, you receive a comforting friend known as the Holy Spirit, who leads you in all truth. The Father, Son, and Holy Spirit are identified as the Trinity. The best description I have read regarding the Trinity I found in *Josiah's Fire*, a book by Tahni Cullen. Her son, Josiah, has experienced many heavenly encounters, and here is Josiah's explanation of the Trinity:

> The Father is the manager. The Son is the lover of operations. Holy Spirit is the worker. So it's the three in one getting things done. The world was created only by three functions that went like this: Father thought it. Son loved it. Holy Spirit carried out the plan. Man must voice, "Father what do you think? Jesus, what do you love? Spirit, what should we do about it?" This is your mission: Do what the Father thinks and what Jesus loves and what Spirit tells.[19]

Sounds pretty simple, doesn't it? Why, then, does it seem so complicated? Because God has given us free will. We get to choose.

Our poor choices and disobedience of God's commands often land us in trouble, which the Bible describes as sin. But when we allow the Holy Spirit to lead us, we can nail our sinful desires to the cross and leave them there: "For it is by believing in your heart that you are made right with God, and it is by openly declaring your faith that you are saved" (Romans 10:10).

God is always at work, readying our circumstances, because he wants to bless us. But we must be willing to wait for his perfect plan to unfold. He will often first purify our motives and prepare our hearts. Other times, he protects us before blessing us. God never makes a mistake; waiting on him will always provide awesome testimony relative to his love, goodness, faithfulness, and provision. Patricia and I met at his perfect time so that God could not only save her life but also save the lives of others, all while demonstrating that nothing can separate us from his love. She and I remain in touch to this day, sending each other cards and letters. And I know that our spiritual connection will endure until we eventually meet again in heaven.

During the summer of 2018, I had planned a visit to the Sunshine State. However, after a routine dermatologist appointment in late May, my doctor detected skin cancer on my right thigh. I pushed out my departure date for Florida by two weeks, underwent a simple outpatient surgery, and then hopped in my car headed south. Scheduled on my trip was a dinner in Jacksonville with Erika Outlaw, a friend and former fellow inmate from Coleman, a stop in Titusville to drop off hundreds of books at the Prison Book Project, and then a drive to Tampa, where two of my friends had moved in together to minimize their expenses. I volunteered to help them downsize and consolidate their households.

I met up with Erika in Jacksonville as planned, and her husband, Chuck, joined us. This was my first time reuniting with a friend from Coleman. Chuck had been a regular visitor at Coleman, and the three of us could not help but laugh at some of the things Erika and I had experienced. Thinking back, Erika might have been the only inmate who did not have a nickname since her surname, Outlaw, was appropriate and hilarious for someone who found herself in prison. Erika was one of my few close friends during my incarceration, and although she had a much shorter sentence than I did, she helped me get through tough times by providing a listening ear, reminding me to focus on the positive, and making me laugh. "You know that's right!" was her signature phrase. We had so much fun reminiscing about our time together, and all of the catching up led to a short night of sleep!

The next morning, I headed south down I-95 toward the Prison Book Project's warehouse in Titusville. I was looking forward to lightening my car's load, as so many books weighed it down that there was hardly room for anything else. Ray and Joyce were happy to greet me when I arrived, and I went straight to unloading copies of *Call Me Vivian* and other Christian books for donation. Once that task was complete, Joyce innocently asked, "Do you need any kids' books?" Shortly after showing me what they had available, we once again filled my car to the brim with thousands of dollars' worth of Christian books and Bibles for children.

Really, Lord? I thought. *I wasn't planning on bringing books back to Wisconsin.* He and I both knew that I needed an empty vehicle to help my friends move and consolidate. If God wanted me to have those resources, then he was going to have to help me find a home for them. But it also felt like he was somehow testing my obedience; he knew how excited I was to clean out my car.

Upon arriving in Tampa, I connected with a friend by the name of Eileen. I had actually met Eileen and her husband, Skip, years earlier while staying with a friend who lived next door to them. God has a habit of moving people around; that way, they're right where we need them when he's ready to fulfill his purposes. It should have not been a surprise that Skip and Eileen now lived around the corner from the home of another friend, where I would be staying for the next month.

As we were catching up, Skip and Eileen mentioned how God had moved their hearts to become part of a new church holding its services at The Underground Network located at the University Square Mall in Tampa. The Underground's mission is to inspire people to surrender their lives to Jesus and to empower communities to discover their God-given mission. And it was through their new church that Skip and Eileen met Damon and Zabrina. Damon was a former inmate who served a twenty-year sentence on drug charges. He and Zabrina, his wife, were in the early stages of establishing a nonprofit organization. Eileen said that she thought I should meet them and offered to coordinate the introduction.

Imagine my delight when I officially met this couple a week later at The Underground. We shared our testimony and visions for what God had called us to do. Damon explained that he wanted to focus on helping inmates develop legitimate businesses, and Zabrina wanted to help children of incarcerated parents. Damon's ministry, Inc. to Inc., is a faith and character-based nonprofit organization that equips currently and formerly incarcerated program participants with the skills and tools to become productive and committed employees, business owners, and community members.

Damon grew up in an impoverished, dangerous housing project in Pensacola. His introduction to the fast money of illegal drug sales happened at the age of nine. Fourteen years later, during what most would consider an extremely successful run in the drug game, Damon was arrested and sentenced to twenty years in prison for drug trafficking and distribution. While serving his time, he watched as brilliant, gifted men were released from prison only to return a short time later. The lack of relatable, effective personal development and educational courses and the limited opportunities in their poor communities kept these men going back to the only thing they knew: hustling on the block.

Damon realized that it was up to him to create an opportunity for a second chance to positively change his life and the lives of other drug offenders. With his renewed faith, passions for entrepreneurship and rebuilding his community, and a lot of studying and preparation, Inc. to Inc. Entresition Services was born.

As Damon talked, God reminded me of The Vivian Foundation's early beginnings. I needed people to come alongside me, to encourage me, and to sow into my ministry. I smiled when I realized that was exactly why God had me in Tampa. Here I thought the primary purpose of the trip was to help my friends move, and I eventually did, but Damon and Zabrina had to witness the hand of God early in their ministry calling. And they found out that God had big plans for them.

Just one day after our initial meeting, God told me to return to Damon and Zabrina's office and empty my SUV. Those children's books that I picked up in Titusville were intended for them all along. The looks on their faces were priceless; Damon and Zabrina were shocked at what God had orchestrated. Without knowing how they were going to get things started, God opened the doors and poured out a huge blessing. They now had thousands of dollars of inventory in Christian books and could begin sowing into others.

The Vivian Foundation also provided more than two hundred fifty copies of *The Joseph Calling* by Os Hillman, which was exactly the kind of resource that Damon needed to start his work with inmates. *The Joseph Calling* helps readers navigate adversity, discover their calling, and fulfill their God-given destiny. The story of Joseph in the Bible is one of my favorites. Joseph was the favored son who was betrayed by his brothers, which led to his incarceration of thirteen years. His journey included hardship, humility, and pain, yet God used Joseph's adversities to fulfill a larger story when he became a spiritual and physical provider to others.

We are all Joseph. It doesn't matter if you are a man or woman, young or old, or wherever you may find yourself; we are all set apart for God's divine purposes. God wants you to know his assignment so that you can live an intentional, meaningful, purposeful life.

11

It was apparent that God had me in Florida for more reasons than one. I attended several ministry meetings that resulted in so many opportunities to bless others. While still in Tampa, I wondered what the next few months would hold, and then God spoke to my heart,

> *There is a level of uncertainty in your life. Continue to trust me. The next season, however short, is a springboard to what's next. While you are being refined, obedience is required. Bask in the love of your family and friends and the joy they bring to your very existence. Balance will be required for successful service. I am moving. Blessings will reign down in due time. My time.*

Although God was showing me that it was time to slow down after five weeks of extremely hard work in Florida, that was easier said than done. Still, I packed up and drove back to Wisconsin but had clearly failed to listen to the Lord's reminder that successful service requires balance. I was so ready to sleep in my own bed that I drove straight though, covering 1,236 miles in nineteen hours and thirty-two minutes.

My next opportunity arrived when I received two pallets of *The 5 Love Languages* coloring books. I immediately thought of Ann Edenfield Sweet, the founder of Wings for LIFE International, another established ministry that The Vivian Foundation supports. I first learned about this organization, located in Albuquerque,

New Mexico, from the Oklahoma senator whom I had met at the CMCA Conference in Atlanta. Although Ann and I had never met in person, God was doing amazing things through the connection of our ministries.

Incarceration touched Ann's life when her first husband received a sentence of fifteen years in federal prison. After navigating the twists and turns that came with his sentence, she authored *Family Arrested: How to Survive the Incarceration of a Loved One.* She began Wings Ministry in 1995 when she came face-to-face with the demands of the judicial system while trying to raise four young sons under challenging circumstances. Ann initiated a second program, Wings for LIFE (Life-skills Imparted to Families through Education), which is an empowerment program that provides life skills, education, training, and support to children and family members of inmates, inmates re-entering society, and at-risk youth. Ann and her husband, Doug, also lead marriage seminars in prisons for inmates and their spouses.

When I called Ann and told her about the pallets of *The 5 Love Languages* coloring books, she was interested. Little did I know that *The 5 Love Languages* by Gary Chapman is one of the books that Ann uses in her outreach program. We both chalked up my call to the Lord. The Vivian Foundation provided thousands of Christian books as well as Vivian Foundation resources for Wings' Easter, Christmas, and back-to-school events, blessing children in a tangible way. I would soon come to understand just how powerful an impact the distribution of these resources can have.

Meet Ryan, a former gang member serving time on heroin drug charges. Ryan began serving his time in a prison in Hobbs, New Mexico, but was awaiting a transfer to a maximum-security penitentiary in Santa Fe when he sent me a letter. He shared how God had put it on his heart to write to me after he learned about The Vivian Foundation from a "Just One Word Bible Reading Plan" that someone had placed under the door of his cell.

Like I do with every inmate who writes me, I shared words of encouragement and mailed my reply. A short time later, I received his response: "Never did I imagine that the author of a book and president of a foundation would write…I started crying tears of joy, and I dropped to my knees and started thanking God, yelling at the top of my lungs, 'God is not dead! He is surely alive.' "

I told Ryan I would send him a copy of *Call Me Vivian*, but he was privately worried that he wouldn't receive it. The correctional captain had told him that The Vivian Foundation was not an approved vendor, and all Christian books must be mailed to the chaplain of the prison with the inmate's name included on the package. Ryan considered writing me to warn me of this hurdle, but something told him to rely on his faith instead.

Soon after, Ryan saw the chaplain and said, "Hey, I was going to ask you if you could be on the lookout for a package from The Vivian Foundation."

"You mean this one?" the chaplain said, holding up the package.

Ryan could not believe it. He told God that he did not deserve this type of favor. Both Ryan and the chaplain thanked the Lord for his divine intervention, and let's just say that God had a few more surprises for all of us. Once Ryan was well into reading my book, he discovered my personal connection to a woman by the name of Ruth Ann Nylen.

"No way!" he exclaimed aloud.

Back when Ryan was first put in segregation to await his transfer to Santa Fe, a church volunteer at the Hobbs prison visited and told Ryan, "I have a book that God told me to give to you." The volunteer told Ryan that it was the only copy his ministry had, but he wanted Ryan to have it anyway. The book was *The Radical Power of God* by Ruth Ann Nylen.

The night that he received Ruth Ann's book, Ryan was feeling "pretty lost and discouraged," nearing his breaking point. "I was thinking about my whole life, and I broke down crying. I looked at Ruth Ann's book, picked it up, and started reading it. It hit me hard...and it referred me to the 'Just One Word Bible Reading Plan,'" which we know had been placed under his door by an unknown angel. By God's divine design, the good Lord was showing Ryan just how powerful God truly is.

Ryan told me he had sent a letter to Ruth Ann, thanking her. "She didn't realize that book saved my life, as I was in a state of mind that left me wanting to take my own life. I was blown away. What are the chances that you were working with Ruth Ann prior to your surrendering to serve your time, and what are the chances that everything aligned so perfectly?"

You'd have to read *Call Me Vivian* to know how important Ruth Ann was to my personal transformation and how faithful she was in visiting me while I served my time. Today we sit on each other's board of directors for our respective ministries, and we continue to work side by side to spread the good news of Jesus Christ. Together, we obediently dropped off resources at the Prison Book Project in Titusville, Florida, in June of 2016. God had clearly taken care of the rest.

In another letter to me, Ryan wrote, "Your book blew me away. I read it in two days...I came to tears at least ten times and stopped counting after that." He hated to admit it, but he worried that his displays of emotion had put his prison reputation at stake. Ryan went on to share that the *Call Me Vivian* books that I had sent to his family were already making a difference, too, and he reminded them, "All you need is faith and love, and God will cast our prayers up to dance with the stars."

Aloud, Ryan wondered how he could reach the world and use his story to help save God's people. Well, this former lost sheep and tough guy clearly had an epiphany while serving his time. He penned this powerful prayer to the Lord and kindly shared it with me.

Everything that has happened in my life has been my own doing. I have no reason to justify who I once was. But I didn't want the ruins I left in my path to be in vain...It is in our sin that you truly listen and speak the truth, but it's when we hear silence that you are preparing the truth of your greater purpose and divine work...It is in the silence that we must remain ever so faithful to your divine purpose. To your moments of silence, I will forever respond with faith and love, so I may gratefully await the task at hand. It is your faithful nature that takes the initiative to accomplish all you set out to do in our lives. For this I pray in the righteous name of Christ. Amen.

Two months later, I received another letter from Ryan telling me he had arrived at the penitentiary in Santa Fe. He shared that he was prepared to face any obstacle thanks to his newfound faith and was happy to report that his appearance had changed drastically since his time on the streets—so much so that some of the inmates who knew him previously did not recognize him. His demeanor had changed too. A friend of his commented, "I don't ever remember you smiling."

The new Ryan signed up more inmates for Bible study than ever before, including a man from California whose reputation preceded him. "He was a radical inmate," Ryan wrote, telling me that *Call Me Vivian* had brought this hardened man to tears. Ryan also told me that he remembered what I would say whenever people would say things like, "Let me guess: You went to prison and found Jesus." I would reply, "I didn't know Jesus was lost!" But Ryan has a more thoughtful response for these people.

God placed Moses and his people in the wilderness for forty years because despite all they had seen, they were still defiant...The desert consists of rocks, sand, and mountains, and prison is a form of wilderness with stone, metal, chains, and little to see yet so much to see if we are willing to ask the Holy Spirit to open our eyes.

When people go through hardships, struggles, affliction, abandonment, and loneliness, they are all a form of wilderness, all a form of God, all a form of our very salvation…I truly believe God will let us experience the impossible if we choose to see it and live it. For example, the world is taught that there is only one moon to light up the night, but for me, I've learned that there are many moons in my life to light up my darkness.

Ryan and his testimony moved me deeply. To him and others like him, I have two important things to share. First is Daniel 12:3: "Those who are wise will shine as bright as the sky, and those who lead many to righteousness will shine like the stars forever." The second thing I want to share was written by Daniell Koepke, author of *Daring to Take Up Space.*

If I've learned anything from life, it's that sometimes, the darkest times can bring us to the brightest places. I've learned that the most toxic people can teach us the most important lessons; that our most painful struggles can grant us the most necessary growth; and that the most heartbreaking losses of friendship and love can make room for the most wonderful people.[20]

Katie Souza, a former federal inmate, runs another ministry to which The Vivian Foundation has provided copies of *Call Me Vivian*. When I was incarcerated, an inmate had placed a book of hers, *The Key to Your Expected End*, under my pillow in my cell. Within this book is a prophecy by Bill Yount titled "Prisons Hold God's Treasures" from his book *I Heard Heaven Proclaim*. This prophecy offers powerful hope to inmates. In it, Yount recounts how the Lord told him about people in prisons and jails, who "have almost been destroyed by the enemy, but these ones have the greatest potential to be used and bring forth glory to My name…Tell My people that great treasure is behind these walls, in these forgotten vessels."[21]

Yount's vision continues, detailing how the Lord then freed his people with a universal key before Jesus joined the throng of inmates, who glowed silver and gold from Jesus' touch before growing in size and becoming "giant knights" clad with the armor of God—every piece made of solid gold. The warriors were then placed at the front lines of battle, delivering God's people from Satan's clutches.

Also brought into God's house in Yount's prophecy were the "rejects of society, street people, the outcasts, the poor and the despised."[22] The Lord concluded Yount's vision with a message telling people that they are needed in the streets, hospitals, missions, and prisons, where God's people can find him and where they will be judged by his Word in Mathew 25:42–43.

> For I was hungry, and you didn't feed me. I was thirsty, and you didn't give me a drink. I was a stranger, and you didn't invite me into your home. I was naked, and you didn't give me clothing. I was sick and in prison, and you didn't visit me.

Jesus demands our personal involvement in caring for others: "Share your food with the hungry! Provide for the homeless and bring them into your home! Clothe the naked! Don't turn your back on your own flesh and blood!" (Isaiah 58:7 TPT). Or as Hebrews declares it so clearly and eloquently, "Remember those in prison, as if you were there yourself" (Hebrews 13:3).

I had been reflecting on these verses and how The Vivian Foundation and I personally could do more for others when I started dreaming about "apple dares" in early November 2018. An apple dare, as explained in *Josiah's Fire*, is something that happens in heaven. Josiah describes it like this:

> The apple dare factory is the factory of God's rich opportunity to do something you normally wouldn't do. You get an apple…to take to earth in angel helpers' hands to a person that needs to take a dare…dares are in apples, for instance, because they are sweet rewards to those who pick them…The person begins to feel a strong desire to take a daring leap… that makes them need God more to accomplish such a feat.[23]

Later that month, I booked a trip to Tampa, where my board members live, to hold The Vivian Foundation's board of directors meeting. *Call Me Vivian* was finding its way into unlikely places, and doors began to open. For example, our partnership with Treasured Pearls, a ministry based out of Tampa, was set to begin soon. We were providing this ministry with copies of *Call Me Vivian*, devotionals, and The Passion Translation Bibles that would be distributed to exotic dancers in strip clubs. Tampa ranks third in the nation for its number of strip clubs per capita.[24]

While we discussed our other priorities for 2019, my board members told me that I had too much time on my hands and needed a job. I flatly refused their suggestion, stating that my time in corporate America was over. "If I do anything," I proclaimed, "it's going to be ministry work to help advance the kingdom of heaven."

A few days later, I received my very own "apple dare" when my cousins announced that my aunt Dorothy needed a full-time caregiver. Since they're family, I was aware of their circumstances. At almost eighty-eight years of age, aunt Dore had breast cancer that had metastasized to the bone. I immediately asked God if this is what he had in store for me and decided to go for a walk while I awaited his answer. It didn't take long for him to confirm with his presence that he wanted me to spend this time with my aunt. My cousins were grateful when I called to tell them that I would help, and my aunt was both thrilled and relieved that someone she knew would be involved in her care.

Her birthday is January 27, which lines up with a verse in the book of James: "Pure and genuine religion in the sight of God the Father means caring for orphans and widows in their distress and refusing to let the world corrupt you" (1:27). I had started my apple dare in late November, and within a week, I received a sweet reward: an unexpected monetary gift from my family. The love I provided had an unexpected reward, and that is often the case when we look closely.

A few years ago, I delivered a speech titled "Love Makes the World Go Round." I chose this title because I had been humming that very song by Deon Jackson for weeks, and around that same time, God had put a few books in my hands, including *Why Am I Afraid to Tell You I'm a Christian?* by Don Posterski, *How to Give Away Your Faith* by Paul Little, and *How Jesus Treated People* by Morris Venden. At the same time that I was reading these books and preparing my speech, I came across a quote of Helen Keller's, and the Holy Spirit prompted me to take a closer look at her life.

Born on June 27, 1880, Helen Keller was a healthy infant. At nineteen months of age, she contracted a serious illness that left her deaf and blind. At the age of six, her mother took her to the Perkins Institution for the Blind, where the school's director asked a twenty-year-old former student, Anne Sullivan, to become Helen's instructor. By age twenty-four, Helen graduated from Radcliffe College, becoming the first deaf and blind person to earn a Bachelor of Arts degree and then going on to become a world-famous speaker and author.

We can learn many important lessons from Helen Keller and Anne Sullivan, but what I would like to focus on are Helen Keller's words of wisdom. She said many profound things, but this one is among my favorites: "There is no better way to thank God for your sight than by giving a helping hand to someone in the dark." What makes this quote powerful is that it echoes God's desire for all of his people to experience the world fully, and despite becoming blind and deaf as an infant, Helen Keller not only learned to speak but also became a world-famous speaker—during an era in which deaf people were considered "imperfections in the public body" no less![25]

As I had learned from Venden's book, Jesus was a man of the world too. The son of a businessman, Jesus' interactions with his father's customers gave him the necessary skills to relate to all kinds of people. As he moved out of carpentry and into the business of building God's heavenly kingdom, he was at ease moving within an array of social settings and circles. He was comfortable among tax collectors, government officials, and prostitutes, and he was more concerned with human dignity than social status.

Crossing cultural barriers, Jesus reasoned with the religious elite in the morning and preached to people in the streets in the afternoon. Rather than calling on people to come to him to hear him speak, he stepped out and went toward them, opening the door to himself. He is our model, which means we need to follow his example. And his marching orders to his disciples were clear: Go where I have gone and do what I have done! This, too, is our objective: to walk in obedience and let others witness the light of Christ shining though us.

I see this light shining through my grandsons. In the fall of 2019, I made two separate trips to Minnesota to attend my grandsons' cross country meets. It was so fun to see all three boys run in their respective meets. Colin, a freshman at the time, was on the junior varsity team while Nicholas, a senior, and Ben, a junior, were among the top runners on the varsity team. Personally, I give a lot of credit to anyone who runs cross country. Running 3.1 miles on hilly terrain in the scorching heat at the beginning of the season and freezing temperatures by the end of the season…let's just say that would not be my first sport of choice. That fall also marked Nick's last season, and he had been running varsity since the eighth grade. Ben's improvement throughout the season was quite impressive, too, and both qualified for the state meet.

I could see God's favor manifesting itself in all three of their lives. He had blessed each of them with an abundance of competitiveness, strength, endurance, and humility. Nick, for example, ranked either number one or number two throughout the entire season and was the top returning senior at Minnesota's state meet. But given the way he carried himself, you would never have known the success he achieved. Instead, he let his results speak for themselves. He did not go undefeated, but his second-place finish at the state championship that year remained etched in the record books. Ben finished strong as well, and his running future looks bright.

When I saw both Ben and Nick after the state championship meet, they were pleased with their times and finishing places, yet

Nick said, "Grandma, I had a little left in my tank. I should have gone with the leaders." I was proud that he knew exactly what he needed to do to improve. And in my heart, I knew how he felt. It brought me back to my senior year of high school when my basketball team placed second in the state championship. When we are willing to look at our lives objectively and sincerely want to improve, great things can and will happen. This rings equally true in athletics and in the journey of life.

The next weekend, all three boys ran in the Nike Heartland Regional race in Sioux Falls, South Dakota. Eight regional meets were held throughout the country, and only the top five individual runners in each race would qualify for the Nike Cross Nationals held in Portland a few weeks later. I chose to follow the regional race online, as the one- and two-mile results posted in real time. When the two-mile standings posted, I read my laptop screen and saw that Nick was in eighth place. I started praying, asking God to give Nick the strength and endurance to win the race. When the final results posted, Nick had moved up seven spots and won the race! It was a personal best time, and Nick advanced to the national meet in Oregon.

In less than four and a half minutes, God answered my prayer. And it was not lost on me that the number seven represents completion and perfection in the Bible. Once again, God received the glory, and I believe he used this race to reward Nick for his humility. It was a much bigger win than the previous week, and with it, he defeated the state champion from Minnesota, who had beaten him earlier that season. In three short weeks, Nick would board a plane with the rest of the family and head to Nike Headquarters in Portland, where they treated him like royalty, whisking him around to all kinds of fun activities with other qualifying runners and outfitting him in Nike clothing before he competed in the most prestigious cross-country race in the nation.

The national meet was broadcast live, which was a blessing considering the cold temperatures and pouring rain endured by those in attendance. Nick finished in 31st place, and all I could say was "Thank you, Jesus." He received the accolade of 2019–2020 Gatorade Player of the Year in Minnesota for Boys Cross Country and headed to the Air Force Academy to continue his running career. The craziest part is that when he was five years old, he drew a picture of an Air Force plane, which we saved and put in a scrapbook. He had spoken this success over his life long before any of us knew the trajectory of his life.

I am indescribably proud of the fine young men that Nick, Ben, and Colin have become, both in the classroom and in their extracurricular activities. Ben, whose senior cross country season was cut short because of COVID-19, bounced back and enjoyed an outstanding track and field season the following spring. At Minnesota's state track and field meet, he finished second in the 1,600-meter race and third in the 3,200-meter race, setting two personal records that year. Ben is now a collegiate runner, following in his older brother's footsteps. Colin continues to improve each season, too, due to his hard work and dedication. He has come a long way since middle school, when he performed a leading role as Donkey in his school's *Shrek the Musical*. The sky is truly the limit for these three. Of course, God ultimately gets the glory for them and their success, but my son, Mike, and his former wife, Kelly, deserve tons and tons of credit for having raised three astounding kids together.

The Bible tells us in Hebrews 12:1–2 to "run with endurance the race God has set before us. We do this by keeping our eyes on Jesus, the champion who initiates and perfects our faith." Similarly, 1 Corinthians encourages us to "run to win" and "with purpose in every step" (9:24, 26). The Christian life is no different than the life of an athlete. It demands hard work, self-discipline, and preparation. We are running toward our heavenly reward of eternal life. God promises that we will reap a harvest of blessing if we don't give up. No matter where you find yourself or what the circumstances, God works all things for good for those who love him and are called according to his purpose.

12

As the calendar turned and 2020 began, I felt relieved to leave 2019 behind. Although our family was delighted to celebrate a great cross-country season for the boys, it had proved a tough year overall. My mom had been hospitalized twice; my dad suffered a heart attack, and my brother, Joe, passed away after battling numerous health issues over the summer.

I did not mind my caregiving role. It was an honor and a privilege to serve my family in that capacity, but I struggled to understand why the Lord was keeping me in this season for so long. Still, I could see God's hand in many things that had happened, and many rewarding ministry moments took place, but my spirit was growing restless. And I was tired.

Caregiving is hard work and, quite frankly, with everything we had endured, I was ready for a change. The feeling reminded me of how I felt more than ten years ago, when I volunteered at a nursing home in Tampa for two years as part of our church's Homebound Ministry team. Many of the elderly women I assisted were instrumental in transforming my heart, and I wrote about this experience in *Call Me Vivian*. But when I least expected it, the desire of my heart changed, and I no longer wanted to be there. Assuming something was wrong with me, I brought my concerns to my Bible study group.

"Guys, I think something is wrong with me. For two years I have been volunteering at the nursing home and enjoying every minute of it. I'm so good with the ladies, and they love me. But now, all of a sudden, I wake up and cannot even stand the thought of driving over there. What the heck is wrong with me?"

"Nothing," said one of the members in my group, laughing. I was dumfounded until she went on to say, "God is changing the desire of your heart. He has something else for you to do."

She was right; God was stirring up my heart again, forcing me to confront another part of my character. He's good at that. In my experience, these moments of confusion and searching often mean that God is preparing to move me into a deeper, more fulfilling experience in my walk with him. He is always at work in our lives—leading us, teaching us, and revealing his next opportunity for us. And over the past few months, I had received numerous letters from inmates asking when book two would be available. My response remained consistent: "I am not going to start writing until the Lord tells me it's time."

Then on May 13, 2018, God gave me the title and subtitle of this book, *Vivian's Call: A Labor of Love*. In January and over three consecutive nights, God gave me the same three numbers: eight, sixteen, and nineteen. I scoured the Bible, trying to figure out which passages he wanted me to read but found nothing relevant to my current situation. Then the Holy Spirit prompted me to look up the biblical meanings of those numbers. The number eight represents new beginnings, sixteen represents spiritual wisdom, and nineteen represents faith. I hoped the Lord was telling me that I had finally acquired the spiritual wisdom that was necessary to step out in faith and embrace a new beginning.

God had also given me one particular Scripture verse at least a dozen times: "At the right time, I, the LORD, will make it happen" (Isaiah 60:22). I knew I had to stay the course. And as 1 Peter reminded me, "Care for the flock that God has entrusted to you. Watch over it willingly, not grudgingly—not for what you will get out of it, but because you are eager to serve God. Don't lord it over the people assigned to your care, but lead them by your own good example" (5:2–3). God wants us to serve others in love, and the first attribute of a true servant is humility. These individuals are gentle and show compassion. They love to encourage others, and they possess a passionate appetite for righteousness. They are also merciful, pure in heart, and sincere and honest in their motives. Servants also tend to be accepting, tolerant, and positive, and, typically, have patient endurance.

Obedience and servanthood go hand in hand. They both require personal involvement and Christlike selflessness. God remembers every act of service, no matter how big or small. He knows our hearts and sees the love behind our actions. He sees everything we do and will reward us for those good deeds.

My caregiving role continued into March of 2020 as our family prepared to welcome my first granddaughter into the world. Quite honestly, I wanted to spend time with my grandchildren rather than work. However, the Lord clearly told me to commit to the gift, which meant I would most likely continue to care for my aunt until the fall.

McKenzie Jo entered this world the second week of March, weighing an impressive nine pounds and five ounces. She was over twenty-one inches long, and the size of her hands already has me looking forward to the day when she receives a college basketball scholarship. This perfect little miracle of a girl also has her mother's feet, which means she'll have some God-given talent when it comes to playing soccer. Kenzie is an absolute cutie pie and resembles her twin brothers, who love and adore her. And with three children under the age of three, my daughter and son-in-law have their hands full.

Just a week after Kenzie's birth, I received additional encouragement from the Lord, who whispered, *You are going into a season of abundance. The key is patience.* God's timing is always perfect, yet we sometimes become impatient waiting for him to act. The good news is that he sees our passion for the plans he's placed in our hearts and loves our enthusiasm. We run farther and soar higher when we wait patiently for him, so we must believe that no matter how long the season, he will bring us the sweetest of rewards for trusting his perfect plan. And at the right moment, he will make it happen and ensure our success.

During the last weekend of March, I was running a fever and not feeling well. With the COVID pandemic in full swing, I called my cousins on Saturday and told them I thought it was best to take off the first week of April as a precautionary measure, given my aunt's compromised immune system. They agreed. Two days later, I read a social media post about Nostradamus. I found that both interesting and unusual, as I had read his book, *Les Propheties*, while incarcerated. Nostradamus was a French astrologer, physician, and reputed seer from way back in the 1500s. He wrote a series of predictions for future events, and I wondered what the Lord was trying to tell me.

I grabbed my printed copies of the emails I had sent while in prison and started reading through them. It was interesting to look back at my correspondence, and I was surprised when I realized how much of *Call Me Vivian* was written from prison. As I turned the pages, I did not find anything on Nostradamus, but I knew with certainty that I had discovered exactly what God intended me to find. See, I had been struggling to figure out how to begin this book. How could I write an introduction to a story that was playing out in real time? Of course, in my old emails, God had provided the momentum I needed to begin writing.

I texted my friend Paula that I was happy to report that God had birthed book number two. It did not take long for her to respond. Just a few minutes later, she said the Holy Spirit was screaming, *It is time! It is time!* Now covered in goose bumps (which I actually refer to as "God bumps"), I had to call her, because just a few pages earlier in my prison notes, I had read this sentence: "As my friend Paula always says, 'It's time.'"

"The thought of having to write this while caring for my aunt is going to difficult," I told Paula over the phone. "When God writes through me, I can type for six or seven hours at a time. Having to break up my day with her care could be problematic."

And as I learned last time, it is not unusual for God to wake me up in the middle of the night to write for a few hours, after which I sleep in. I even admitted to Paula that I wanted to call my cousins and tell them I could no longer care for my aunt, but God told me otherwise. "God knows the desire of my heart," I said. "If he wants to free me up to write, he will."

Less than twelve hours after making that statement, I received a phone call from my cousin. She and her brother had been talking and decided it was best for me to take the month off with pay, given the uncertainty of the pandemic. They would assume the role of caring for their mother.

When God wants us to do something, he always makes a way. With confirmation that it was indeed time, I headed to my office, fired up my computer, and typed more than forty thousand words in two days. I could not believe how much content I had, having forgotten so many of the things I had written in my journal. My writing continued through the middle of April. I was excited about the progress I was making, and it was fun to be back in my office with Pandora's "Relaxation Radio" playing in the background.

When I least expected it, God's favor manifested itself again when I received an email from BroadStreet Publishing offering me a deep discount on the remaining inventory of *Call Me Vivian*. This allowed The Vivian Foundation to send a large quantity of books to the Prison Book Project, and the financial savings not only covered the pallet shipping cost to Florida but also allowed me to sow into their ministry with a nice donation.

I also shipped four cases of *Call Me Vivian* to CLI Prison Alliance located in Raleigh, North Carolina. Over the past three years, I have shipped hundreds of *Call Me Vivian* books to their facility for distribution. The Prison Book Project and CLI Prison Alliance complement one another, and together they ship well over five hundred thousand books into correctional facilities each year.

The dedication and hard work of both ministries has *Call Me Vivian* in circulation in nearly three thousand jails and prisons across the country, and another thousand books were shipped to a prison ministry in Australia. Success in ministry and life all comes down to patience, prudence, and providence. If we wait on the Lord and remain good stewards of what he has given us, then God will manage every microscopic detail of our ministry.

Near the end of April, with the second book nearly finished, my phone rang on a Saturday. Caller ID showed me it was coming from Louisiana. Feeling a prompting in my spirit to answer, I was surprised to discover that the person on the other end of the line was none other than TJ, an inmate with whom I had been corresponding for close to a year. The last time I had heard from him, he was awaiting a court date in mid-March. As we chatted, he mentioned his court date had been delayed because courts were closed as a result of the pandemic. Any hopes TJ had of an early release had been placed on hold.

TJ went on to share that he and a few other inmates were told there was a possibility they'd be released early given the spread of COVID-19. Unfortunately, TJ owed a significant amount of money to the state, so his release was unlikely. But a prison administrator approached him a few days earlier and said, "Someone must have been praying for you." Not only was TJ released, but the state also forgave his fines.

"TJ, you just received a miracle," I told him. "I am so happy for you."

This was the first time we had spoken, and it turned out that TJ was calling me from a relative's phone. Prior to that Saturday when we spoke on the phone, we had exchanged close to a dozen letters. He opened up to me in his correspondence and shared the desires of his heart. Our phone conversation that day lasted close to forty minutes, and it was obvious that the Holy Spirit was speaking through me as I shared godly advice with him.

"The devil is crafty, TJ. He does not like the fact that you were released by the grace of God. We know it was God who opened that door and forgave that debt, and it is God who has given you a wonderful opportunity to turn your life around."

We spent a fair amount of time discussing the following Scripture passage: "You can enter God's Kingdom only through the narrow gate. The highway to hell is broad. And its gate is wide for the many who choose that way. But the gateway to life is very narrow and the road is difficult, and only a few ever find it" (Matthew 7:13–14).

TJ understood exactly what I meant and felt strongly that his only chance for success was to get out of Louisiana. He mentioned that he was not sure where he would spend the night but sent me a text a few hours later that read, "God takes care of the lilies of the field and the birds, so I know he can take care of me."

Knowing TJ needed spiritual support and guidance, I reminded him of the importance of surrounding himself with godly people during his difficult time of transition. He asked if I knew of any job opportunities, but given most businesses were closed because of the pandemic, he was in a tough spot. I wished him the best and told him to stay in touch, as I was excited to see what the Lord had planned for his life.

On Monday, I received a text message from an unknown Louisiana number. It had come from a prison. TJ wanted to talk to me. The wind was sucked out of me in a way that made me feel ill. It took one swift Google search to learn that TJ had been arrested for breaking and entering less than twelve hours after we had spoken. TJ's saga continues, and he now has another charge to add to his already lengthy criminal record.

Given the heavy disappointment I felt in my spirit, I sensed God felt that way too. It seemed like he was showing me how he feels every time one of his children turns away from him and heads down the wrong path. I had invested in TJ's life for almost a year. I stressed to him what he needed to do, but he chose to return to his old ways.

We are all given free will, and wherever we find ourselves is often a direct result of our choices. I paged through my Bible looking for an explanation for what had happened with TJ, and God took me to the book of Romans: "Anyone who rebels against authority is rebelling against what God has instituted, and they will be punished…The authorities are God's servants, sent for your good…So you must submit to them, not only to avoid punishment, but also to keep a clear conscience" (13:2, 4–5).

God issued additional marching orders when he said, "Teach them my commands," referring to the Ten Commandments found in Exodus chapter 20. God had spoken to Moses on Mount Sinai and gave him two stone tablets inscribed with the terms of the covenant. Of all the biblical laws and commandments, the Ten Commandments alone were "written by the finger of God" (Exodus 31:18).

I reread the list, pondering what had happened with TJ and why so many people find the commandments difficult to obey. Summarized, the commandments are truly quite simple and written so that even a child can understand them.

1. Love God more than you love anything else.

2. Don't let anything else be more important to you than God.

3. Always respect God's name.

4. Rest on the seventh day and honor the Lord.

5. Respect your mom and dad.

6. Don't hurt anyone.

7. Be true to your husband or wife.

8. Don't take anything that doesn't belong to you.

9. Never tell a lie.

10. Don't be jealous of what others have. Be happy with what you have.

The Ten Commandments, also known as the law, speak of integrity, respect, loyalty, purity, honesty, and contentment. Originally issued to the people of Israel during the Old Covenant, the law's purpose was to guide the Israelites, instructing them on what they should and should not do. The problem was that the Israelites did not possess the spiritual power to obey. You may wonder what that means.

You see, we needed the new covenant that Jesus established and the gift of his Holy Spirit in order to become capable of walking in obedience. The third person of the Trinity, the Holy Spirit, dwells within us once we ask Jesus into our hearts, which is also known as becoming "born again." It is the Holy Spirit who gives us the power to do whatever God requires in terms of our service and obedience. What all of that boils down to is this: We no longer have an excuse for disobeying God's commands. We have both the strength and power to do so.

Not to mention that Jesus clearly tells us, " 'You must love the LORD your God with all your heart, all your soul, and all your mind.' This is the first and greatest commandment. A second is equally important 'Love your neighbor as yourself' " (Matthew 22:37–39). A common question, then, is why the commandments were ever issued if it's impossible for us to be completely obedient. The Bible answers this.

> Is there a conflict, then, between God's law and God's promises? Absolutely not! If the law could give us new life, we could be made right with God by obeying it. But the Scriptures declare that we are all prisoners of sin, so we receive God's promise of freedom only by believing in Jesus Christ. (Galatians 3:21–22)

In short, these verses in Galatians explain why we must be born again. "If you openly declare that Jesus is Lord and believe in your heart that God raised him from the dead, then you will be saved. For it is by believing in your heart that you are made right with

God, and it is by openly declaring your faith that you are saved" (Romans 10:9–10).

When I returned to work the last week of April, my aunt's decline was noticeable. It appeared that it would only be a matter of time before she would need additional help. The decline in her health was so reminiscent of my brother's. I did not want to go through the heartache and pain of losing another family member so soon. I knew that was the real reason I wanted my season of caregiving to end.

But at age eighty-nine and with her disease progressing, my aunt admitted she was "getting old," and although we never talked about it, we both knew her time on earth was winding down. She asked me what I thought her late husband was doing, and I knew her thoughts were on the two of them reuniting.

On my last day of caring for her, a cardinal perched on her patio for a long time. I took it as a sign from heaven that everything was going to be okay. I had mixed emotions when the family took over her daily needs, yet I knew in my spirit that it was time for me to step away. God had work to do in the hearts of those entrusted with her care. As I walked out of her apartment that last evening, she simply said, "Thank you so much for everything."

When I returned home, I sat in tears in my bedroom. I had responded to God's call and poured everything I had into caring for my aunt for the last eighteen months. And we had so much fun throughout that year and a half. I had forgotten how funny she was; her one-liners were hilarious! I called two of my friends for moral support.

One said, "Kate, your aunt had a good run."

"You were such a blessing," the other chimed in. "You poured godly love into her in a way that only you could. God saw everything you did, and your heavenly reward awaits you. Take comfort in knowing that you helped her stay in her own home, and you provided companionship that made the end of her life so much more enjoyable."

I knew that everything they said was true, but that did not make saying goodbye any less painful. When someone you love is preparing to leave this life and venture into the next, a little part of you goes with them every day. Still, God taught me so many things throughout that challenging season of hospitals and loss. I learned that the greatest gift you can give another person is your time. When you give them your time, you give them a portion of your life that you will never get back. And God's love is brought to its full expression in us when we love others as he loves us.

Mark Twain once said, "The two most important days in your life are the day that you are born and the day you find out why." I was born in May of 1957, but I didn't know the call that God had placed on my life until October of 2011. That was when he confirmed that I was to give him all the glory by becoming an author and sharing my heavenly experiences and testimony with others. He also directed me to start The Vivian Foundation. Since then, Acts 20:24 has become my signature verse: "My life is worth nothing to me unless I use it for finishing the work assigned me by the Lord Jesus—the work of telling others the Good News about the wonderful grace of God."

On April 11, 2021, the Lord clearly told me, *The true mileage we travel will be based on the strength of our resolve.* The strength of your resolve is your determination, which is a positive emotional feeling that involves persevering toward a difficult goal in spite of obstacles. Tough, difficult times have made me more confident and determined to succeed. And true determination is a spiritual quality that's acquired by yielding to the Holy Spirit and to God's will. However, we can't reach our goals without God's help.

By his divine power, God has given us everything we need to live a godly life. We have received all this by coming to know him, the one who called us to himself by means of his marvelous glory and excellence. And because of his glory and excellence, he has given us great promises. These promises enable us to share in his divine nature and escape the world's corruption caused by human desires (2 Peter 1:3–4).

Our sinful nature wants to do evil, and when we follow those desires, the results are clear: sexual immorality, impurity, lustful pleasures, idolatry, sorcery, hostility, jealousy, outbursts of anger, selfish ambition, dissension, division, envy, drunkenness, and other sins like these. Let me tell you again, as I have before, that anyone living that sort of life will not inherit the kingdom of God.

The Holy Spirit produces love, joy, peace, patience, kindness, goodness, faithfulness, gentleness, and self-control. Know that the sinful nature and the Spirit are forces that are constantly at war with each other. So let the Holy Spirit guide your life. He will protect you from giving in to whatever it is that your sinful nature craves.

Let me ask you this. If someone wrote a book about your life, what would the title be? Would you be happy with your story up to this point in time? More importantly, on judgment day, do you want to hear God say, "Well done my good and faithful servant," or "I never knew you"? (See Mathew 25).

God gave us free will, and he will honor your decision. I personally chose to experience the power and purpose of God's glory in my life, and I've never looked back because God works everything together for the good of those who love him and who are called according to his purpose for them: "God knew his people in advance, and he chose them to become like his Son, so that his Son would be the firstborn among many brothers and sisters. And having chosen them, he called them to come to him. And having called them, he gave them right standing with himself. And having given them right standing, he gave them his glory" (Romans 8:29–30).

God wants to make your story a bestseller, but you must embrace his perfect plan for your life and step out in faith: Faith is the confidence that what we hope for will actually happen (Hebrews 11:1). "It is impossible to please God without faith. Anyone who wants to come to him must believe God exists and that he rewards those who sincerely seek him" (Hebrews 11:6). Faith is complete trust and loyalty to God, and it yields a willingness to do his will. It is complete and humble obedience to him and a readiness to do whatever he asks.

When Jesus' time on earth was coming to an end, he and his disciples went to Gethsemane to pray. Jesus bowed his face to the ground and prayed for his Father's will to be done. He resolved to do things God's way even though it meant terrible suffering. Jesus died so that we could live life to the fullest. His purpose was to give us a rich and satisfying life (John 10:10). He became the final, ultimate sacrifice for sin and finished God's work of salvation with his own death on the cross. Jesus answered God's call. The question is, *will you*?

Nothing can separate us from God's love, and *Vivian's Call* has proven that your happily ever after is closer than you think. You can't change the beginning of your story, but you can start right now and allow God to be an integral part in the remaining chapters of your life. All you need is a willing heart; God always takes care of the rest.

Acknowledgments

To my Lord and Savior, Jesus Christ: Thank you for handpicking me for this assignment. Thank you for the miraculous transformation of my heart and for the strength and courage to trust your perfect plan. I ask that you continue to direct my steps and open doors for my good and your glory. Your abundant blessings are a testament to God's grace and goodness.

To my family and friends: Thank you to my family for your love, support, and patient endurance while God prepared my heart for ministry. I love you. To my sister Nancy, who assists with foundation requirements, I am so glad that God chose you to be an accountant and not me! To my Bible study group in Tampa, the journey continues.

To my ministry partners: Thank you for your tireless service to bless those impacted by incarceration and your prayerful support of The Vivian Foundation. Special thanks to Ruth Ann Nylen and Really Good News Ministries for partnering with us, and to both Ruth Ann and Paula Aghoian for their faithful service as board members.

To BroadStreet Publishing and their team: Thank you for providing The Vivian Foundation one hundred thousand-plus Christian books, which have been shared among prison ministries and other nonprofit organizations throughout the country. Our partnership and this book ministry was part of a greater plan that only God could have orchestrated. Nina Rose, I am forever grateful for your editing expertise and God-given talent as we perfected my story.

To Ray and Joyce Hall and all of the volunteers at the Prison Book Project: Thank you for helping me realize my dream of getting at least one copy of my book into every jail and prison that your organization supports.

To Jack and Scottie Barnes of Forgiven Ministry Inc., their staff, and volunteers: It was an honor and privilege to serve alongside you at "One Day with God." I was forever changed by my experience at the North Carolina Correctional Institution for Women in Raleigh. Thank you for your many years of faithful service and for answering God's call.

To Sandra Kearns of On Wings Like a Dove, Ann Edenfield Sweet of Wings for LIFE International, and CLI Prison Alliance: It's been a pleasure to partner with you to help inmates and families of the incarcerated.

To the local ministries that The Vivian Foundation supports (including Youth for Christ of Southeastern Wisconsin; Faith, Hope and Love for Kids in Racine; Teen Reach Adventure Camps; Safe Haven; The Salvation Army of Southeastern Wisconsin; and Community Warehouse): Thank you and your volunteers who have helped bless more than one hundred thousand individuals with Christian books.

To those who have financially sown into The Vivian Foundation: Thank you for your faithful giving and supporting our cause. We have touched well over one hundred fifty thousand lives both inside and outside of prisons with our resources.

To the many inmates who have contacted me: Thank you for sharing how God has used my testimony to encourage you and speak to your heart. He gets the glory! Your prophetic words continue to amaze me and have helped me stay the course.

I would especially like to thank those inmates whose stories were included in *Vivian's Call.* You are now touching countless lives with your testimony. Well done!

Endnotes

1   Spencer Johnson, *Who Moved My Cheese?: An Amazing Way to Deal with Change in Your Work and in Your Life*, 2nd ed. (New York: G.P. Putnam's Sons/Penguin Putnam Inc., 2002), back cover.

2   *Merriam-Webster*, s.v. "agnostic," accessed February 6, 2016, https://www.merriam-webster.com/dictionary/agnostic.

3   Pamela Gerloff, "You're Not Laughing Enough, and That's No Joke," *Psychology Today*, June 21, 2011, https://www.psychologytoday.com/us/blog/the-possibility-paradigm/201106/youre-not-laughing-enough-and-thats-no-joke.

4   *Merriam-Webster*, s.v. "repent," accessed March 7, 2016, https://www.merriam-webster.com/dictionary/repent.

5   Wendy Sawyer and Peter Wagner, "Mass Incarceration: The Whole Pie 2020," Prison Policy Initiative, March 24, 2020, https://www.prisonpolicy.org/reports/pie2020.html.

6   From A. J. Russell, *God Calling* (Uhrichsville, OH: Barbour Publishing, 1989), 64–65. Used by permission.

7 "About," Correctional Ministries and Chaplains Association, accessed July 1, 2016, https://www.cmcainternational.org/about/.

8 *NLT Parallel Study Bible* (Carol Stream, IL: Tyndale House Publishers, Inc., 2011), 2352.

9 Aesop, "The Tortoise and the Hare," *Short Stories: East of the Web*, accessed August 2, 2016, http://www.eastoftheweb.com/short-stories/UBooks/TorHar.shtml.

10 "Children and Families of the Incarcerated Fact Sheet," Rutgers University, accessed May 28, 2015, https://nrccfi.camden.rutgers.edu/files/nrccfi-fact-sheet-2014.pdf.

11 Brooks Faulkner, "7 Biblical Models of Leadership," Lifeway, September 8, 2015, www.lifeway.com/en/articles/church-leadership-seven-biblical-models.

12 *Lexico*, s.v. "escape," accessed March 30, 2017, https://www.lexico.com/en/definition/escape.

13 *NLT Parallel Study Bible*, 2570.

14 *Merriam-Webster*, s.v. "admiration," accessed January 7, 2021, https://www.merriam-webster.com/dictionary/admiration.

15 Kevin Leman, *The Birth Order Book: Why You Are the Way You Are* (Ada, MI: Revell, 2009).

16 Dorothy Law Nolte, "Children Learn What They Live," EmpowermentResources.com, accessed September 3, 2018, http://www.empowermentresources.com/info2/childrenlearn-long_version.html.

17 "Death Row," Death Penalty Information Center, accessed December 15, 2021, https://deathpenaltyinfo.org/death-row/overview.

18 "Types of Empathy," Skills You Need, accessed April 22, 2020, https://www.skillsyouneed.com/ips/empathy-types.html.

19 Tahni Cullen and Cheryl Ricker, *Josiah's Fire: Autism Stole His Voice, God Gave Him a Voice* (Racine, WI: BroadStreet Publishing Group, 2016), 170.

20 Daniell Koepke, "If I've Learned Anything from Life…," Internal Acceptance Movement, accessed May 14, 2020, https://internal-acceptance-movement.tumblr.com/post/45275008001.

21 Bill Yount, *I Heard Heaven Proclaim* (Hagerstown, MD: McDougal Publishing, 2004), 50, 51.

22 Yount, *I Heard Heaven Proclaim*, 52. Capitalization of quotation has been altered for readability.

23 Cullen and Ricker, *Josiah's Fire,* 196–197.

24 Angie Drobnic Holan and Katie Sanders, "Is Tampa the 'Strip Club Capital of the World'?" PolitiFact, January 13, 2012, https://www.politifact.com/factchecks/2012/jan/13/ellyn-bogdanoff/tampa-strip-club-capital-world/.

25 *Encyclopaedia Britannica Online*, s.v. "History of the Deaf: The 19th Century," accessed December 17, 2021, https://www.britannica.com/science/history-of-the-deaf/The-19th-century.

About The Vivian Foundation

The Vivian Foundation is a 501(c)(3) nonprofit charitable organization established in 2015 to help the children of incarcerated parents. Our mission is to raise money and provide Christian resources to children with incarcerated parents, to prison ministries, and to other nonprofit organizations dedicated to helping these families.

The American criminal justice system holds almost 2.3 million people in 1,833 state prisons, 110 federal prisons, 1,772 juvenile correctional facilities, and 3,134 local jails. There are 2.7 million children in the United States who have a mother or father behind bars, and approximately ten million children have experienced parental incarceration at some point in their lives. Will you prayerfully consider sharing God's love and supporting our mission to help inmates and their children?

The Vivian Foundation is dedicated to improving the well-being and quality of life for these individuals and doing whatever it takes to positively impact these families. Please visit our website at www.thevivianfoundation.com. Tax deductible donations can also be mailed to: The Vivian Foundation PO Box 44601, Racine, Wisconsin 53404–7012.